BEGINNER'S
GUIDE
FOR THE
UCSD PASCAL
SYSTEM

by Kenneth L. Bowles

Subsidiary of McGraw-Hill
BYTE BOOKS   **70 Main Street**   **Peterborough, NH 03458**

Library of Congress Cataloging in Publications Data

Bowles, Kenneth L.   1929-
  Beginner's manual for the UCSD Pascal Software System.

  Includes index.
  1. UCSD Pascal Software System (Computer system)   2. Pascal (Computer program language)   I. Title.
  QA76.6.B69   1980   001.6'425   79-23467
  ISBN 0-07-006745-7
  10   9   8   7   6   5

Table of Contents

Appendices

1 Overview

1.1 Who

This book is intended to be used as an introduction and reference manual for people just beginning to use the University of California, San Diego (UCSD) Pascal Software System. The book is designed to be used by at least the following three groups of people:

- College students, high school students, and others who have never before used a computer.
- Experienced programmers who have not used UCSD Pascal, particularly those who have been using BASIC and those not yet familiar with interactive, video display-based, programming systems.
- Nonprogrammers who intend to use packaged programs designed to run within the UCSD Pascal System.

Some portions of the book are designed for use by only one or two of these groups and can readily be scanned or ignored by others.

Our intent is to make it possible and facile to learn to use the UCSD Pascal System by working just with the book and a small computer. You may find it useful to obtain assistance from someone already familiar with the UCSD Pascal System, but that help should not be necessary.

1.2 What

If you are a beginner, and do not recognize the terms used in this section, you may wish to skim over the rest of this overview chapter and turn directly to chapter 2, Orientation For Beginners.

The UCSD Pascal Software System is a complete, general-purpose software package for users of microcomputers and minicomputers. Some of the principal features of the UCSD Pascal System are as follows:

- In general, programs written to run on the UCSD Pascal System are portable (ie: they may be run on many different small computers without being altered). The UCSD Pascal System is much more portable than most large software systems. At this writing it is being used on machines based on the following processors and systems: the PDP11, 8080; 8085; Z80; 6502; 6800; 9900; AM-100; the Western Digital Microengine; and the General Automation GA16 family of minicomputers.
- The UCSD Pascal System is designed to make it easy to develop and use programs on a small, single-user computer with a television or similar display screen and with one or more floppy-disk drives for secondary storage. If you intend to use the UCSD Pascal System to develop programs, you will need at least 48 K bytes of programmable memory. With the volume marketing of 64 K bit memory devices expected to start in 1979, the size of memory required to run the UCSD Pascal System should cease to be a major cost consideration for most users.
- Though designed for program development, the UCSD Pascal System can also be used for many special-purpose applications. Examples include: word processing; computer-assisted instruction (CAI); interactive business-data processing; communications; process control; and scientific analysis. When the computer is not to be used for program *development*, it is often possible to operate the UCSD Pascal System with much less memory space than the 48 K to 64 K bytes needed to develop programs.
- While designed primarily for use with programs written in the Pascal programming language, the UCSD Pascal System also allows work with other languages.

This book concentrates on features of the UCSD Pascal System intended for all users including beginners and students. The many advanced features of the UCSD Pascal System are described in a separate reference manual written for experienced programmers.

1.3 Pascal

Pascal is a powerful, general-purpose programming language designed by Professor Niklaus Wirth of the Technical University in Zurich Switzerland. The language is named in honor of Blaise Pascal, a famous seventeenth century mathematician. However, mathematics is by no means the only field in which the Pascal language is found to be useful.

The standard Pascal language, consisting of Wirth's definition published in 1971 and a few corrections made since then, was originally introduced to help in teaching a systematic approach to good program design. You may have heard of a method known as *structured programming*, with which professional programmers are able to write large and complex programs in a manner that avoids many of the errors that plague programming work in older languages like BASIC, COBOL, or FORTRAN. Among the practical and usable programming languages currently in widespread use, Pascal is the best statement of what structured programming is all about.

Pascal is coming into widespread use for writing complex programs in most fields where computers are applied to practical problems. For these applications, the standard Pascal language is often extended to provide specialized facilities not present in Wirth's original definition. There is no widespread agreement on what extensions may be needed for practical applications of Pascal. Instead there is a growing feeling that the number of extensions to the language should be kept to a minimum in the interests of greater program portability between dissimilar machines.

Virtually all of the UCSD Pascal System is programmed using a slightly extended version of the Pascal language that we will call UCSD Pascal in this book. UCSD Pascal includes most of the standard language, and, up to the limits of small computers, it is faithful to the standard language. Once a forthcoming international standard for the language is approved by the International Standards Organization (ISO), the UCSD Pascal will be revised to eliminate as many of the remaining differences as practical. The extensions beyond the standard language in UCSD Pascal have been included to facilitate teaching, by the use of nonmathematics-oriented problem examples, and to facilitate writing a variety of large interactive programs on small computers. A close approximation to the standard Pascal language definition may be found in *Pascal User Manual and Report*, by K Jensen and N Wirth (Springer Verlag, New York NY, 1975).

UCSD Pascal is relatively easy for beginners to learn, as proven by the thousands of students who have completed an introductory problem-solving and computer-programming course at UCSD. It is probably true that beginners can learn to write very small programs slightly faster using BASIC than they can using Pascal. As soon as the beginner reaches the stage of needing more than a very few GO TO statements, learning to solve the same problem using Pascal becomes easier. Thereafter, the larger the program, the greater the advantage will be to use Pascal instead of BASIC. Most people who are familiar with both Pascal and BASIC agree that any extra effort to learn Pascal is repaid as soon as they try to write a large program.

1.4 How to Use this Book

This book is designed to be used both as an orientation guide for people who are first learning to use the UCSD Pascal System and as a reference manual for the same people once they are familiarized with the UCSD Pascal System. As a reference manual, this book contains enough information to assist in a wide variety of advanced applications of the UCSD Pascal System. However, advanced users with a serious interest should probably supplement this book with the detailed reference manual (available from most distributors of the UCSD Pascal System software and from some computer stores).

If you have not used computers before, or if your experience is with an old system such as those using punched cards for input, you probably should start reading this book in Chapter 2, Orientation for Beginners. If you have written programs before using some language other than Pascal, and if you have used an interactive computer facility, then you probably can start in Chapter 3, Orientation for Experienced Programmers. To avoid any more duplication of text than necessary, Chapter 3, Orientation For Experienced Programmers, is also intended to be read by beginners who have already read Chapter 2.

Whether you are a beginner or an experienced programmer, you will find this book easier to use if you have ready access to a microcomputer on which you can work with several sample disk files designed specifically for use with this book. These include the program ORIENTER, which may be supplied to you with the name SYSTEM.STARTUP, and the text files EDITDEMO, and COMPDEMO. Since all versions of the UCSD Pascal System have not been distributed initially with these files, you should check with your supplier to make sure that these files are included with your copy of the system software on diskette.

Whether you are learning to program using Pascal or just learning to use the UCSD Pascal System, you should concentrate on the earlier portions of Chapter 4, Screen Editor, and Chapter 5, File Manager. These are the portions of the UCSD Pascal System with which you will be spending most of your time. The screen editor and the file manager are major tools for facilitating your use of the UCSD Pascal System. Both chapters present the most frequently used commands in an order designed for beginners to quickly make practical use of the UCSD Pascal System. Since this order does not lend itself to convenient reference use of the book, summaries of the commands are also given in Appendix C.

If you are learning to program the computer by using Pascal, you should be using the Pascal self-study quiz programs. These quiz programs are designed to be used in association with the textbook *Microcomputer Problem-Solving Using Pascal*, by K L Bowles, (Springer Verlag, New York NY, 1977). There is a quiz program associated with each chapter of that textbook. If you are using the textbook in a college or school course, you will probably be asked to show mastery of the material from each chapter by passing its quiz. Even if you are studying Pascal without involvement in an organized course of instruction, I strongly recommend that you use the quiz programs until you master the material they present. Time spent to understand the material of the earlier chapters of the textbook will help you save time to work through the later chapters. The textbook lacks instructions on how to use the UCSD Pascal System or the quiz programs. Chapter 7 of this guide gives general instructions on how to use the quizzes. Chapter 8, Programming to Use Disk Files, of this guide describes how to write Pascal programs which use disk files under the UCSD Pascal System, a subject not treated in *Microcomputer Problem-Solving Using Pascal* cited above.

The UCSD Pascal System provides a method of augmenting the Pascal language for specialized programming applications using separately prepared libraries of routines. As this book was being completed for publication, the facilities for working with these libraries had only recently been completed. It is expected that programmers will soon be able to choose from a rich and expanding repertoire of library routines to simplify programming for many common applications. Chapter 9, Using Libaries of Specialized Routines (Units), describes how to use library routines in the UCSD Pascal System. Directions on how to use specific libraries of routines will generally be packaged along with the disk or any other medium used to distribute the routines.

Though the UCSD Pascal System is designed to be used on a wide variety of small computers, extensive use is made of several common control keys that are not always found on the keyboards of low-cost microcomputers. In this book, I cope with this problem by asking you to make believe that these special keys actually exist in your keyboard. The effects of these keys can usually be simulated using combinations of other keys. Instructions for using the real keys to get results as if you had the imaginary special keys are given in Appendix A for small computers and in Appendix B for video-display terminals. If the machine you are using is not mentioned in Appendix A or B, the equivalent reference information should be available from your UCSD Pascal System supplier.

2 Orientation for Beginners

2.1 Goals for this Chapter

- Familiarize yourself with the computer you plan to use, with its keyboard and with the method of inserting your floppy disk to get the UCSD Pascal System started (called bootloading).
- Learn what it means to use a *command* directing the computer to do something.
- Distinguish between single-character commands and commands that ask for data.
- Distinguish between a series of commands and a *program*, the latter being a series of commands stored in the computer's memory in such a way that those commands can be repeated upon request.
- Learn how to translate the important, abstract control commands used throughout this book into actions you need to perform using your computer to implement those commands.

2.2 Getting Started

[Note: *This chapter is designed to be read when you have a computer next to you and can use the computer immediately to try out the steps described in the book. To do this exactly as described in the book, a copy of the file ORIENTER.CODE stored as SYSTEM.STARTUP must be on the disk with which you bootload your computer. If your computer does not react as described in this chapter, check with your supplier of the UCSD Pascal System (eg: computer store, instructor, etc.) to make sure that you have the files designed for use with this book.]*

If you are like most people when they first start to use a computer, you probably do not know what to expect at this point. If someone who has already used the UCSD Pascal System is available to help, a demonstration would be beneficial to cover the material of this chapter and the next. Lacking someone to demonstrate in person, I will give you step-by-step instructions so that you can become familiar with the system on your own.

An unfortunate problem that we have to confront from the beginning is that not all small computers are identical, which makes getting started more confusing to a beginner. Appendix A and Appendix B contain information on several computers and terminals to help you use UCSD Pascal in spite of differences among small computers. Read through the rest of this section completely *before* referring to Appendix A or B.

First, I assume that your computer has been turned on and is functioning correctly. Carefully insert your diskette (the one containing files associated with this book) into the lowest numbered disk drive connected to your computer. On a machine with only one drive, there is no confusion about which drive has the lowest number. On a machine with two or more drives, they are generally numbered starting at 0 (ie: 0, 1, etc.). See Appendix A for specific instructions on how to identify which drive has the lowest number, and how to insert your diskette into that drive.

[CAUTION: The floppy disk can be damaged or ruined if not handled carefully! Dust picked up off a table through one of the slots in the protective jacket can often ruin a disk. The disk can be ruined if your write on it with a ball-point pen; if you fold the disk or jam it under the cover of a three-ring notebook; if you leave fingerprints on the disk itself by holding one of the slots in the protective jacket; or if you toss it around like a Frisbee. All these precautions may suggest that you should have second thoughts about getting involved with computers in the first place. Actually, it takes just a little effort to take care of your diskettes. When you do, they can last without damage through years of frequent use.

Both the disk and the computer might be damaged if you insert the disk into the disk drive in the wrong direction. Out of the eight different ways in which the disk might be inserted into the drive only one is correct. The protective envelope, within which the actual disk is stored, is generally marked on one side with a printed label. With most computers, the correct orientation of the disk is the one achieved by holding the diskette with your right thumb on the printed label, or at least holding the same side of the diskette envelope.

You hold the diskette with the labelled side nearest to you, (ie: so that the printing appears upside down to your eyes). On some machines, the disk is inserted in a horizontal position, on others it is vertical. See Appendix A, or other specific instructions for your machine, regarding this point.]

Once the diskette is safely in the disk drive, and the door closed, you may have to take some additional action to get the UCSD Pascal System started. In the jargon of the computer industry, the process of getting the system started is called *bootstrap loading* or simply *bootloading*. When you bootload, essential parts of the UCSD Pascal System are copied from the diskette into the active memory of the computer's central processor unit. On some machines, you can begin bootloading automatically by closing the door of the disk drive after you insert the diskette. On others, you need to press a separate switch or button to initiate the bootloading process. It may be necessary to press one or more keys on the keyboard in some specified sequence to initiate bootloading on certain machines. Again, see Appendix A or other specific instructions for details regarding your machine.

If the bootloading process is successful, the result will be one of the following:

- an announcement on the display screen that the UCSD Pascal System is running
- a displayed figure very similar to display 2.1 shown in the following section of this chapter

What if you get neither result? On some machines, you can detect whether bootloading is proceeding correctly by listening to clicking noises from the disk drive. On others, an indicator light may go on while information is being transferred from the disk into the computer's memory. On still others, you may get no detectable indication that the transfer is going properly and you will have to wait 15 seconds or more to determine whether the transfer is properly completed. I dwell on this point mainly because occasionally problems arise with computers. In most cases, you should experience no problem in bootloading the UCSD Pascal System for the first time. If something does go wrong, it is advisable to go back through the steps that got you to this point, to make sure that you have not forgotten something or to ask for help from someone acquainted with the use of the UCSD Pascal System.

2.3 Simple Commands

When you first unpack the UCSD Pascal System disk associated with your copy of the system, it may already be arranged to produce display 2.1 as the result of bootloading.

If, instead, you get a display with a message similar to the following in the middle of your screen:

WELCOME APPLE0, TO
U.C.S.D. PASCAL SYSTEM II.1
CURRENT DATE IS 15-JUL-79

you can get the Maze output of display 2.1 by the following steps:

- Press the X key on your keyboard. The computer should respond with "EXECUTE WHAT FILE?" in the top line.

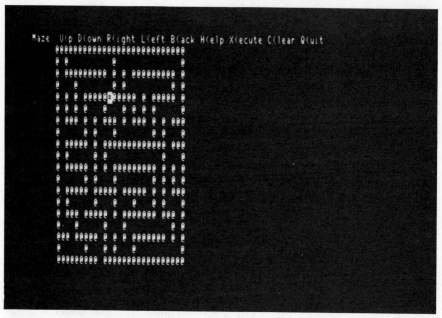

Display 2.1: Initial display for Maze exercise. Throughout this book, where appropriate, we have actual photographs of the display screen of a computer running the UCSD Pascal System to illustrate various points.

- Type "ORIENTER" and then press the RETURN key. If the computer responds with the Maze program output of display 2.1, you can ignore the remaining steps in this list. If the computer responds with "NO FILE ORIENTER.CODE", it is time to insert a disk marked as associated with this book in place of the disk you used to bootload the system. On most computers running the UCSD Pascal System, this disk will be put into the left or lower numbered diskette drive, Pascal unit number 4.
- Again press the X key. When the computer asks "EXECUTE WHAT FILE?", type "#4:ORIENTER" and press the RETURN key. This last step should be successful even if all the others fail. If not, you may wish to try the same sequence of steps several times before seeking expert assistance.

The display that appears on the screen of your computer may differ slightly from that reproduced here in display 2.1. For example, your screen may not be wide enough to show all of the characters on the top line of the figure. This is not a serious problem, as the top line is intended as a reminder which can just as easily be taken from the illustrations in this book.

Now direct your attention to the character "#" displayed just five lines below the character R in R(ight), which is on the top line of the screen. The display consisting of barriers made out of "@" characters is a maze. In the exercise associated with this display, you will go through the steps necessary to find the exit from the maze, starting at the point marked with the character "#". The object of the exercise is to give you concrete examples and practice with what we call a *command* in computer jargon.

[Note that the character "#" on your computer's screen differs from the same character printed in display 2.1. Depending upon the model of computer or computer display terminal that you are using, the character "#" may be marked as an underline character "___". It may be marked by being displayed as a dark character on a light background, or the reverse if all other characters are dark on a light background. The "#" may be blinking on and off once or twice each second or it may be marked by some combination of these methods. Whatever the method, the marker is known in computer jargon as a cursor, and the character that is marked is said to be located at the cursor position. I have not marked the cursor position in the figures in this book, since it is awkward to print the cursor in a way that suggests all of these marking methods at once.]

Now press the D key on your keyboard once. The result should be the appearance of the character "+" immediately below the "#" character. At the same time, the cursor position should move to mark the newly created "+". A single D character will also appear near the bottom left side of your screen.

[If nothing at all happens on the screen in response to your pressing the D key, chances are that you have not pressed it hard enough! **Note:** *if you press the D key again at this point or if you inadvertently pressed it more than once, the bell or buzzer on your computer will sound off. If that did not happen, do not be afraid to press D again just to see what it sounds like. The bell is frequently used as a signal to warn you that you are attempting to use a command that does not make sense at that particular time.]*

Next, press the R key twice. The cursor should move two boxes to the right, placing additional "+" characters on the screen as it goes. If you press R a third time, the bell will sound again signifying that you are trying to bump into another wall. Press D once or twice, and the result should be to move the cursor down an equal number of places, again leaving "+" characters on the screen.

By this time, you can see that you command the computer to do something each time you press the D or R key. Note in the top line of the screen that there are command characters associated with all four directions in which the cursor can move within the maze. D stands for down, R stands for right, L for left, and U for up. The top line is used as a reminder about the available command letters, and what they are supposed to do.

The "(" character used with each command word is a reminder that only one character needs to be pressed to initiate the associated command. When using some other computer systems, you need to type in the whole word to initiate a command. This is not the case when using the UCSD Pascal System.

Try your hand at finding your way out of the maze. The only way is at the open box along the bottom line of the maze. Display 2.2 shows the result of taking a shortcut, which is obviously wrong. Do not let the beeps of the bell, or buzzer bother you. They simply tell you that you can not keep moving in the direction indicated by the command letter you have just used.

Next, if you have not already done so, it would be a good time to see what the B(ack command does by pressing B. If you have moved from the starting

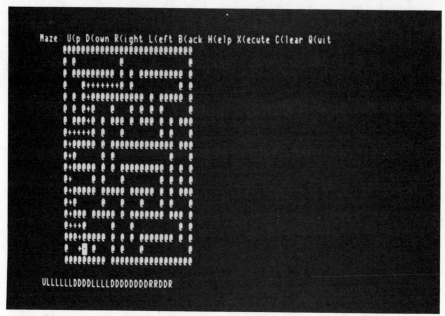

Display 2.2: A bad way out of the maze. Starting with the initial position as shown in display 2.1, one series of L, R, U and D commands results in moving to this position in the maze. The position is marked by the solid square with a dark line in it, at the lower left of the display screen. The sequence of commands used to get to this position is seen as a line of letters across the bottom of the screen.

position of the "#", each press of B will remove one "+" from the screen, backing you up toward the starting point. You may already have noticed that none of the commands U, D, R, or L will allow you to back over a "+" already placed on the screen. Press H to see what the H(elp command does. The maze will disappear off the screen, and a list of brief explanations of the available commands will appear. You can return to the maze display by pressing the SPACEBAR key, the long thin key at the bottom of your keyboard (ie: the one closest to you). The C key, the C(lear command, restores the maze display to the condition it was in when you first bootloaded. The eX(ecute command is explained in more detail in section 5 below. If at this point you press the Q key for Q(uit, it might be best to start over by bootloading again. I will explain in more detail what is going on in a later section.

2.4 Special Keyboard Characters

All keyboards used with computers have at least some characters designed to be used for special purposes. I am not ready to show you all of the special control characters. However, I can begin at this point with a few of the characters used for moving the cursor around on the screen.

Not all computer keyboards have special keys for all of the control commands that are used frequently in the UCSD Pascal System. The exercises associated with this chapter are designed to give you practice with the special control keys, if they are present on your keyboard, or otherwise practice with sample ways to *simulate* the action of these control keys. As a result, it is advisable at this point for you to scan over the section of Appendix A or B, or the equivalent documentation for your machine covering Special Keyboard Characters.

2.4.1 Return

As a starting exercise, go through the maze as in the previous section leaving a dozen "+" characters in the maze. As before, the B key causes you to back up toward the starting location each time it is pressed. Now press the RETURN key (marked as CR or RET on some keyboards) and note what happens. We have arranged things *for this exercise alone* so that the RETURN key is an alternate method for invoking the B(ack command. The RETURN key is used commonly for several other purposes throughout the UCSD Pascal System. For now, we just want you to be familiar with the RETURN key itself.

2.4.2 Control

Notice that your keyboard has at least one key marked CONTROL, or sometimes CTRL. Two keys are used together to create the same effect on the Radio Shack TRS-80 (see Appendix A2). This key is similar in effect to the SHIFT key of most keyboards, in that CONTROL changes the effect you get from pressing many of the keys on the keyboard. In the Maze exercise, if you press the M key the computer will simply beep at you signifying that it has no corresponding command. Now, hold down the CONTROL key, then press M while still holding CONTROL down. Note that what happens is the same as when you press B or RETURN. Explanation: each key on the keyboard, when pressed, sends a unique coded message to the computer. If you hold down SHIFT, the message may change, as from lowercase "a" to uppercase "A." If you hold down CONTROL, the message changes so that each key showing a letter has some special meaning that cannot be expressed by showing a single character on the screen. One can arrange the computer to interpret CONTROL+letter messages as calling for a command to be invoked, just as we have used simple letter commands in the Maze exercise. It is often confusing to remember the association between a CONTROL+letter combination and the command action it is intended to invoke. Therefore, most computer keyboards provide a few specially labelled keys which send the same messages as the associated CONTROL+letter combinations. Practically every computer keyboard has a RETURN key. For that reason, we do not have to remember that the same effect can be obtained using CONTROL+M. Your keyboard *may* have specially labelled keys for all the other important control commands used with the UCSD Pascal System. On the lowest priced machines, the manufacturers have saved on cost by eliminating some of the special control keys. If you have one of those machines, you will have to learn to use the CONTROL+letter combinations described in Appendix A, or alternative instructions for your machine.

2.4.3 Arrow Keys for Moving the Cursor

Now, go back through the Maze exercise using the special CONTROL commands for up, down, right, and left. On some keyboards, these commands are associated with four special control keys marked with arrows pointing in the four directions. On others, only the left and right arrows are provided. Still others have no arrow command keys at all for positioning the cursor. You will need to memorize the CONTROL + letter combinations associated with up, down, left, and right if their corresponding command keys are missing. It may help to tape notes to your keyboard to remind you which CONTROL + letter combinations are used to simulate the missing special command keys.

A few words about context may help you to understand what we have been doing here. You may wonder why we need the special CONTROL + letter combinations at all if the command letters U, D, R, and L will work just as well. The answer is that we have arranged for those letter commands to work as described just within the Maze exercise. In using the UCSD Pascal System, you will see that we go from the context or environment of one world to that of another quite frequently. A little later in this chapter, we will switch to another world in order to illustrate how you use commands that require data. Thus far, the commands we have been using are all invoked just by pushing one key, or the equivalent CONTROL + letter combination. Since there are only twenty-six letters in the English alphabet, there are not enough single letter commands to cover all of the things we want to do in different worlds within the UCSD Pascal System. Even if there were enough letters, you would not want to spend the time to memorize all the letter/command associations. The UCSD Pascal System has been designed to make use of some of the commonly available special control keys in order to simplify the use of the UCSD Pascal System as much as possible. For beginners, it is unfortunate that the lowest priced machines often lack some of these keys.

2.5 The Concept of a Program

People involved with computers use the term *program* with several slightly different shades of meaning. We too shall have to do the same in this book. Basically, a program is a sequence of commands stored in the computer in such a way that each command in the sequence can be carried out automatically, (ie: with no help from the operator to go from one command to the next). Generally, the first command in the sequence is carried out, then the next, and so on in the order the commands appear. Methods are available to alter the sequence of commands automatically under certain conditions. Discussion of those methods is best left until you study the Pascal language for writing programs.

In the Maze example, the sequence of command letters appears in the lower part of the screen in the order in which you type them, from left to right. When more than one line is needed to hold a complete sequence, the command letters go from the right end of one line to the left end of the next, as in the presentation of English text. The Maze program can automatically carry out each command shown at the bottom of the screen, since it is also stored in the computer's memory. Once you have several "+" characters deposited in the maze, press the X key and wait to see what happens. The cursor first jumps back to its original position at the "#" character. Next the cursor follows the same route that you followed when you first put the series of "+" characters on the screen. The rate at which it does this is deliberately slowed down so that you can see the correspondence between the position of the cursor within the maze and the command character marked in the command sequence simultaneously.

The sequence of command characters at the bottom of the screen is a crude program. When you press X (for eXecute), the program is executed. To *execute* a program is basically the same as to *run* the program (although the Pascal System, like many others, makes a fine distinction between execute and R(un as we shall see in the next chapter). Both terms are used to describe what happens when a sequence of stored commands is carried out automatically one-by-one. Generally, it is possible to cause a program to be executed as many times as one wishes without altering the program as stored in the computer's memory.

In general, the symbols that we use to represent each command are assigned arbitrarily and purely for convenience. If we spoke Spanish rather than English, "right" would be "derecha," "down" would be "bajo," "up" would be "arriba," and "left" would be "izquierda." It would therefore be convenient to change the letter assignments which correspond to movement of the cursor in the Maze example (eg: instead of "R" for "right," we would use "D" for "derecha," in fact, the meaning of the letter D would change!). Thus the command letters must be regarded as codes which are assigned to shorten the amount of input information necessary to order that a given command "action" be carried out.

The program we have been considering here, in connection with the Maze example, is, of course, a simpified analogy to the programs one finds on most computers. The computer's *hardware*, which you can touch or pick up, generally understands command codes expressed as small numbers. The command actions called for by those codes are typically very simple in concept. Even the simplest of the popular microprocessors now in use has roughly seventy different commands with their corresponding codes. A program that carries out any useful function usually consists of many hundreds or even thousands of these simple commands. Fortunately, most people who use computers have no need to work directly with the numbered command codes. Instead, we write our programs in a form that looks much closer to a sequence of English-language statements. A translator program, called a *compiler*, then converts the humanly readable form of the program into the coded sequence of commands that the computer hardware can understand. The form that most people use today for writing programs is called a *high-level language*. In such a language, the form we use is at a substantially higher level than simple, coded commands of a machine language. Pascal, BASIC, COBOL, and FORTRAN, are all commonly used high-level languages.

In the UCSD Pascal System, a command that you tell the computer from the keyboard to carry out is usually expressed by pressing a single key. In Pascal and other high-level languages, a program more often consists of English words mixed with special characters which represent commands. The English words are used to make a program more readable than a tightly packed sequence of single-character commands like the program displayed at the bottom of the screen in the Maze example. When you are issuing commands to the computer from the keyboard, you are generally aware of the context since the result obtained from issuing each command is apparent immediately. Thus, effort is saved by not requiring that whole words be typed into the computer to initiate the execution of each command. When you read a computer program on paper or on the screen, many commands are lumped together without obvious and immediate connection with the actions they cause when executed. In this context, the readability is much more important than the immediacy afforded by the single-letter encoding of the interactive commands. Interactive commands are those you use when you interact directly with the computer rather than waiting for a program to run.

2.6 Building Bigger Programs out of Smaller Programs

You may have noticed that we used a single-letter command, X, to call for the program of moves through the maze to be executed. In effect, the Maze example is a simulation of a very simple computer designed for a special purpose. It happens that the simulation is a program written in the Pascal programming language which is arranged to respond to the various command letters we have been describing in this chapter.

There is nothing to prevent us from deciding to assign a different command code letter to each of several different programs. Thus X might cause the execution of one sequence of commands taking us toward the true exit of the maze, Y might be another program which goes off toward a dead-end in the maze, and Z might refer to yet another dead-end program. In fact, each of the command letters assigned in the Maze program actually calls for the execution of a small program designed to carry out a specific, simple action.

Obviously, if we can build a program out of any sequence of command codes and can give that program another unique code, it must be possible to build large programs from small programs. In other words, we can create a set of special-purpose commands by writing *low-level* programs (ie: simple ones) to carry out those commands. We can then create a *higher-level* program (ie: one that is larger, more capable, or more complex) by using a sequence of commands each of which calls for execution of one of the low-level programs. We can then create an even higher-level program by using a sequence of commands from the next lower level, and perhaps also from the lower levels within the same sequence. This point is one of the main study goals of Chapter 2 in the Bowles textbook cited in Chapter 1 of this book.

2.7 Commands that Ask for Data

Assuming that you are still working the Maze example on the computer, now press the Q key for Quit. The result should be as shown in display 2.3. This example is designed to illustrate how to use commands that ask for data in the UCSD Pascal System. It also provides a simplified orientation to the use of built-in facilities for working with *strings* of characters in the UCSD Pascal language.

Display 2.3: Initial display for a data-oriented command example.

The general idea of this example is that commands are provided which allow you to alter the phrase "ROW ROW YOUR BOAT" displayed in the middle of the screen. You can I(nsert additional characters wherever the arrow symbol displayed on the next lower line happens to be pointing. You can move the arrow left or right using L and R as in the Maze example. You can D(elete characters starting at the position where the arrow points by typing one X character for each character you want deleted from the displayed phrase. Notice that this is a completely different definition for the D command character compared with its use in the Maze example. There should be no confusion since we are now in the Data example's world rather than that of the Maze example. The first line of the display serves as a reminder of what the Data world's commands are.

2.7.1 I(nsert

Try using I(nsert to obtain the result shown in display 2.4. Do not worry if you cannot easily use *lowercase* characters instead of capitals. We use lowercase here to make the illustration more obvious.

When you press I for the I(nsert command, a message appears on the display screen asking that you type in the characters you want inserted. The cursor waits immediately following this *prompting* message. When you type characters they appear on the screen starting at that point. You can back over characters typed in error by using the BACKSPACE (or simply BS) key if one exists on your keyboard. If you have no BACKSPACE key, the equivalent command action usually can be obtained using the combination CONTROL+H. (See Appendix A or B for your machine if in doubt.) Once the characters typed in are equal to what you intended, you cause those characters to be transferred to the program controlling the I(nsert command by pressing the RETURN key. You should then notice that a copy of the characters you typed in has now appeared within the phrase displayed in midscreen.

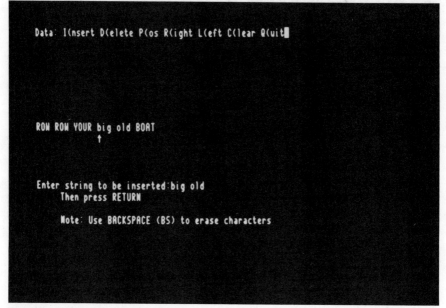

Display 2.4: Displayed string with additional data inserted.

2.7.2 D(elete

The sequence of actions you employ to have D(elete take effect is very similar to that just described. In this case, the D(elete command asks that you type one X character for each character you want deleted in the displayed phrase. Again, BACKSPACE can be used to erase excess characters from the screen. RETURN causes the D(elete command action to be completed. Display 2.5 shows the appearance of the screen just before RETURN is typed to cause deletion of the string "YOUR" from the display. Try this same operation with your computer to observe what happens.

2.7.3 P(osition

The Data example also offers a command for finding the position of a short pattern string of characters within the string displayed in midscreen. Press P to see what happens. The computer will then ask for you to type in the string of characters you want to be found. As an example, type "BOA" followed by RETURN. The pointer arrow on the display should move to point to the "B" at the beginning of "BOAT."

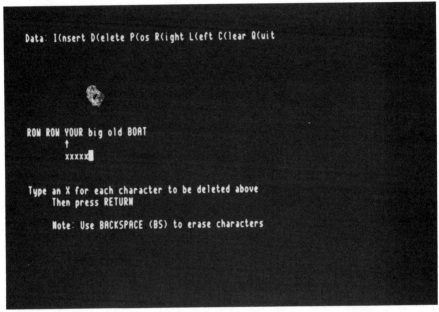

Data: I(nsert D(elete P(os R(ight L(eft C(lear Q(uit

ROW ROW YOUR big old BOAT
       ↑
       xxxxx

Type an X for each character to be deleted above
   Then press RETURN

   Note: Use BACKSPACE (BS) to erase characters

Display 2.5: Appearance of display just before pressing RETURN in the D(elete command.

2.7.4 Summary of the Data World Example

In the UCSD Pascal System, virtually all commands that require you to supply data are handled like the commands in the Data example. Press the command code key and a new *prompt* appears on the screen asking for data. Type in the string of characters, usually a name or a number, and then press RETURN. The command action is then carried out.

As pointed out earlier, commands expressed in the Pascal language generally have the appearance of English-language words instead of single characters. Remember that earlier we described a *program* as a sequence of commands stored for later use. In a program, commands that require data must have that data supplied as part of the program. Unless the program is specifically designed to pick up data from the keyboard, it is generally necessary to store the data needed by the commands as part of the program itself. The manner of supplying the data needed for the Pascal commands is described in Chapters 1 and 2 of the Bowles textbook cited earlier. In that book, the Turtle program, which is available on computers that have graphic display capability, is designed to illustrate the form of using Pascal program commands that require data.

3 Orientation for Experienced Programmers

3.1 Goals for this Chapter

To make effective use of this chapter, you should either have some experience in using an interactive computer system for program development, or you should have studied Chapter 2 of this book.

For most programmers, the principal working environment of the UCSD Pascal System is concentrated in three facilities: the Screen Editor, the File Manager, and the Pascal Compiler. This chapter is intended to give an overall understanding of how the working environment is used. Details on each of the three major facilities are left until Chapters 4, Screen Editor; Chapter 5, File Manager; and Chapter 6, Pascal Compiler—Coping with Program Errors.

Specifically, here is what you will accomplish in this chapter:

- Learn to enter a small Pascal program into the computer, and how to test and run that program.
- Learn how to make simple modifications in a small program already stored on your diskette, and to test and save the modified program.
- Learn what is meant by the *workfile,* and how the Editor, Compiler, and File Manager all cooperate with each other to help manage the Workfile.
- Distinguish between the human readable *text* version of a Pascal program and the *code* version of the same program which is executable by the computer.

- Learn how the File Manager is used as a utility with which you can keep track of your library of program files. Specifically, acquaint yourself with the disk directory as a tool for telling what currently is saved on your disk(s).
- Use the File Manager to change your copy of the UCSD Pascal System so that it no longer implements the orientation program (Maze and Data examples for Chapter 2) when you bootload the system.

CAUTION: *Some of the steps described in this chapter, and involving use of the File Manager, can leave your diskette changed in such a way that it can no longer be used directly with the step-by-step descriptions in this book. If you decide to refer ahead and make random experiments simply to see what will happen, please be prepared for the possibility that you may have to acquire another diskette in order to start again.*

3.2 Brief Overview

In this chapter, I assume that you already know what I mean by a single character *command*, and have a rough idea what is meant by a *program*. I assume that you know how to *bootload* (bootstrap load) the UCSD Pascal System. If in doubt, it would be best to scan through Chapter 2, even if you are an experienced programmer. I also assume that you will be programming in the Pascal language, even though other languages can also be used with the UCSD Pascal System in much the same manner as described here.

The purpose of this section is to give you a quick description concerning how the various major pieces of the UCSD Pascal System fit together. In later sections, I give simple hands-on exercises using the computer with each of those pieces. Depending upon your personal way of doing things, you may find it most effective to go through the quick description first, and then the exercises, or vice versa. In any event, you will save time in using the rest of this guide if you take time to familiarize yourself with the big picture by going through this section.

When you prepare a program to be executed by the UCSD Pascal System, you write program *statements* in a form that can readily be understood by anyone who understands the *programming language* being used. To get the program statements into the computer in a form that the computer can understand you use a large program called the *Screen Editor*. This is provided as a built-in part of the UCSD Pascal System. The Screen Editor is a tool used for purposes similar to those for which you use a pencil and eraser when writing on a piece of paper. There is no practical way for you to write out a program on paper in such a manner that your writing can be directly understood by the computer. Instead, it is necessary to use a keyboard similar to a typewriter, and each key pressed transmits an electronic message to the computer. Without a program to make sense out of the sequences of key-press messages that you send to the computer, those messages would be of very little value. The Editor is the general-purpose program tool that is used to prepare programs for the computer. It can also be used for preparing and editing ordinary written text material, such as this book, as I describe later in this chapter.

The UCSD Pascal System provides two editor programs. I assume here that you are going to use a computer or terminal that has a cathode-ray tube (CRT) display screen, similar to a television screen, and thus will want to use the Screen Editor program. The other editor, called YALOE (for "Yet Another Line-Oriented Editor") is intended for use on *hard copy* terminals, which are much like typewriters. The Screen Editor is much easier to use than YALOE, and provides far more help. YALOE is described in the main system reference manual for the UCSD Pascal System.

The Screen Editor is available in two versions: the standard Screen Editor and the "large file" Screen Editor. The large file (called "L2") version of the screen editor has extra commands needed to handle files on disk which are bigger than the available memory of the computer. Here I also assume that the standard screen editor is being used in the examples of this chapter.

When you use the Screen Editor, the program text or any other material that you are writing is saved temporarily in the computer's memory. I say temporarily because all of the contents of the computer's memory are lost when you turn the machine off, and arrangments are generally made for more permanent storage of the information on a *secondary medium*. Generally, the secondary medium used with the UCSD Pascal System is a flexible diskette, or *floppy disk*. When you finish changing the text of a program with the Editor, and are ready to try it out, you must use the Editor's Q(uit command. The Q(uit command will respond by asking whether you wish to update the version of your text on the diskette or other secondary medium. For simplicity I will only refer to the diskette from now on. If you do request an update, the text stored in the computer's memory will be transferred to the diskette, and stored in an area called the *workfile*.

3.2.1 The Workfile

To understand the purpose of the workfile, it will help to understand how information is stored on the diskette. Information is recorded on a floppy disk using changes in the magnetization of microscopic regions in a magnetic coating on the plastic surface of the diskette. These regions are organized in circular tracks whose purpose is very similar to the grooves on a phonograph record. One diskette has a capacity for at least 90 thousand characters of text. Some recent designs have a capacity for more than one million characters! This space is enough to allow storage of *many* different programs, both in the human readable text form and in the computer executable code form. In order to keep track of all the information which may be on a diskette, the UCSD Pascal System provides a *directory* or table of contents for the information stored on each diskette. The disk directory gives the name of each item, its location on the diskette, how much space on the diskette it occupies, and some additional information needed by the UCSD Pascal System. Each entry in the disk directory refers to a *file* of information stored on the disk. There is a text file for each program, and, in most cases, there will also be a code file. The disk may also be used for storing various other kinds of information. Again, each collection of information referred to separately in the disk directory is called a *file*.

The workfile is just one of many files stored on your diskette. However, its entry in the disk directory uses a special naming convention that saves you trouble while you are working on a new program or changing an old one. When you use the Editor's Q(uit command, and ask for an update, the text you have been working on is saved on the disk under the directory name "SYSTEM.WRK.TEXT". Any older version of the file having the same directory name is removed from the disk when you update in this manner. Whenever you start up the Editor, it assumes first that there is a workfile on the disk and that you wish to work with the text stored in the workfile. The Compiler and File Manager also make assumptions about the workfile that save you from having to take explicit actions to keep track of the file you are currently working on.

3.2.2 Running the Edited Program

Once you are finished making changes in the text of a program using the Editor, you will usually want to have that program changed into the form that can be executed directly by the computer. Then you will want to try the program to see whether it works correctly. This cannot be done until the edited text of the program is translated into the form that will run directly on the computer. The (Pascal) Compiler is a large program provided with the UCSD Pascal System to translate programs saved on the disk in their text form into the equivalent code form which can be executed directly by the computer.

I am glossing over a fine point here. The UCSD Pascal System actually executes all programs using a special interpreter *program, which makes your computer's processor appear to be a processor designed especially for the purpose of executing Pascal programs. This makes it possible to use the same code form of a Pascal program on any one of many different popular processors, including most of those used in microcomputers.*

When you bootload the UCSD Pascal System, you will find yourself in a command world labeled "Command:" at the left of the prompt line at the top of the screen. From the "Command:" world, you use the E(dit command to start up the Editor. When you use the Editor's Q(uit command, the result will be to bring you back to the "Command:" world.

When you first receive the diskette containing your copy of the UCSD Pascal System, the "Maze:" and "Data:" command worlds may always appear first after bootloading. I will give you instructions in a later section of this chapter on how to avoid having the "Maze:" world always appear after using it to get oriented to the UCSD Pascal System. The "Command:" world is what appears when you use Q(uit to get out of the "Maze:" world, and again Q(uit to get out of the "Data:" world.

If you elect to U(pdate the workfile when you use the Editor's Q(uit command, you can request the Compiler to translate the program text stored in the workfile in either of two ways. The most obvious way is to use the "Command:" world's C(ompile command. A shortcut is to use the "Command:"

world's R(un command. The UCSD Pascal System keeps track of what you have been doing to the workfile, and knows whether you have changed the text stored in the workfile since the last time you used the Compiler. When you use the R(un command, and the workfile has been changed, the Compiler is automatically told to translate the text in the workfile. If the Compiler finds no errors in the program, it then saves the code form of the program on the disk, and tells the UCSD Pascal System to go ahead and execute the program. The compiler leaves the code form of the program in the disk file "SYSTEM.WRK.CODE." Thereafter, you can execute the same version of the program over and over again using the "Command:" world's R(un command, without calling the Compiler into action again until you change the text form of the workfile using the Editor. Each time your program finishes executing on the computer, control of what happens returns to the "Command:" world where the UCSD Pascal System waits for your next command.

3.2.3 Saving Workfiles for Future Use

Once you have finished making changes in a program you probably will want to save that program on the disk for later use. You will also want to clear out your workfile in order to work on another program. To do this, you use the "Command:" world's F(ile command, which takes you into the File Manager's world. Most of us have become lazy and refer to the File Manager simply as the "Filer." I shall do so in this guide from now on. The Filer provides commands for saving a workfile under a directory name you may designate, for removing old files no longer needed, for transferring files from one disk to another, for displaying the disk directory on the video display screen, and other file-related commands. As usual, you use the "File:" world's Q(uit command to get back to the "Command:" world.

3.3 Entering and Testing a Simple Program

Next, I will give a step-by-step account of how you enter a simple program into the computer and then compile it and execute it. I will start from the "Command:" world. To arrive there after bootloading, you may have to use the Q(uit commands of the "Maze:" world and the "Data:" world if they are initially provided on your diskette in a form that starts up automatically. In the last section of this chapter, I will show you how to arrange to obtain the "Command:" world directly after bootloading. It would be best not to jump to that point right away, since some familiarity with the UCSD Pascal System gained with a little practice will help you to avoid making an error that could be very awkward to correct.

As subject matter, we will use the sample program STRING1 from Chapter 1, Section 11, of the text *Microcomputer Problem Solving Using Pascal* mentioned earlier. We reproduce that program in display 3.1 as follows:

```
PROGRAM STRING1;
BEGIN
  WRITE('HI');
```

WRITE(' ','THERE');
WRITELN; (*moves to start of next line*)
WRITE ('HI THERE');
WRITELN (' THIS IS A DEMONSTRATION');
WRITELN ('OF PROGRAM EXECUTION');
END.

Display 3.1: Sample program for familiarization with the UCSD Pascal System. This program is taken from the
book Microcomputer Problem Solving Using Pascal, *by Ken Bowles, Chapter 1 section 11.*

You should start from the "Command:" world by typing E for the "E(dit"
command. The screen will go blank and then, after some clicking by the
floppy disk drive, what will appear is as shown in display 3.2.

```
)Edit:
No workfile is present.  File? ( (ret) for no file (esc-ret) to exit )
 :
```

Display 3.2: Appearance of the screen on entry into the Editor. This message occurs when the work file has
previously been cleared with the Filer, or when the UCSD Pascal System is entered for the first time after the
computer's power is turned on.

The prompt line at the top of the screen informs you that you have arrived
in the "Edit:" world. No command options are shown yet, since no workfile is
stored on the disk, and it is necessary to establish one. The second line on the
screen requests that you type in the name of a text file already stored on the
disk, and follow by pressing the RETURN key. In the present instance, you
have no such file to use, so you simply press the RETURN key without typing
in any name. The Editor will respond with the screen display shown in display
3.3, after a short delay accompanied by some more clicking of the disk drive.

```
)Edit:  A(djst C(py D(lete F(ind I(nsrt J(mp R(place Q(uit X(chng Z(ap [E.6f]
```

Display 3.3: Editor's prompt line as it appears when starting an editing session with an empty workspace. The
prompt line contains abbreviated mnemonic reminders of the most common editing operations.

Except for the list of available command characters in the prompt line at the
top of the screen, the display is completely blank. This shows that the working
space used by the Editor in the computer's memory is completely blank. It is a
blank slate on which you can start writing.

3.3.1 The I(nsert Command

To begin typing in the text of the STRING1 program, use the I(nsert command of the "Edit:" world. The somewhat cryptic prompt message that goes
with the I(nsert command tells you that you can start typing the text. Begin

with "PROGRAM" and continue typing until you make a mistake. You can erase a character typed in error by using the BACKSPACE key (see Appendix A or B for an equivalent if your keyboard has no BACKSPACE key). One character is erased for each BACKSPACE character typed and you can back up all the way to the point where the I(nsert command's world was entered. Continue typing after any erasure until you finish entering a section of text that you wish to retain. You can terminate the I(nsert command, while retaining the text typed in, by pressing the ETX key which stands for "end of text"(see Appendix A or B for your keyboard if it has no ETX key).

Within the I(nsert command's world, you move the cursor from the end of one line to the beginning of the next by using the RETURN key. To obtain the two-column indentation in the third line of the STRING1 program example, press the SPACEBAR twice. When you press RETURN to begin the subsequent lines, the cursor will return to the same column indented two spaces from the left margin. This is just what you want until you arrive at the last line containing "END."

To eliminate the indentation for that line, there are several ways of proceeding. I will mention only the most frequently used method here, and leave other suggestions for Chapter 4, Screen Editor. After pressing RETURN at the end of the previous line, the cursor again comes to the third column and waits for further characters to be typed. At that point, you can use the BACKSPACE key to move the cursor to the left edge of the line. Press BACKSPACE only twice to get there. If you press BACKSPACE once more, you will return to the end of the previous line, effectively backing over and erasing the RETURN character from the text as saved in the computer's memory. No harm is done by this action, but when you again press RETURN to get back to the new line, the cursor will again go to the third column.

Now suppose that you have typed in the lines of text shown in display 3.4, which contain several errors. The next question is how to go about correcting those errors without having to start over again.

```
)Edit: A(djst C(py D(lete F(ind I(nsrt J(np R(place Q(uit X(chng Z(ap  [E.6f]
PROGRAM STRING1;
BEGIN
  WRITE('HI');
  WRITE(' ','TREE');
  WRITELN; (* Moves to start of next line *)
  WRITE('HI THERE');
  WRITELN(' THISA DEMSTATION');
  WRITELN('OF PROGRAM EXECUTION)
END.
```

Display 3.4: The contents of the display screen at the end of an I(nsertion which left errors in the text.

Compare the fourth line in this figure with the fourth line in the STRING1 program in display 3.1. In display 3.4, the word THERE is misspelled TREE.

As a first step to correct this, complete the I(nsertion by pressing ETX, if you have not already done so. If you press ETX when you are in the "Edit:" world, the computer responds with an ASCII "bell" to give you an audible reminder that there is no action associated with an ETX in the "Edit:" world. Next, move the cursor so that it points to the character R in TREE. You do this by using the four cursor positioning arrows on the keyboard, or their equivalents for your machine as listed in Appendix A or the manufacturer's documentation. These are the same keys as used for moving around the maze in the example given in Chapter 2 of this book. With the cursor pointing at the R, use the I(nsert command again. Once in the "Insert:" world, type in HE followed by pressing the ETX key. Notice that the I(nsert command in this case moves everything starting with the R over to the right-hand margin of the screen. This is done in order to leave you blank columns into which the additional characters may be typed. When you press the ETX key, the characters moved to the right of the screen will be returned to connect up once again with the portion of the line still on the left side. At this point, the misspelled word has been partially corrected, and should read THEREE.

The following is a summary of what you can do with the I(nsert command:

- You enter the "Insert:" world by typing I while in the "Edit:" world. You can then type in characters of text starting from the cursor's position (as it was when the "Insert:" world was entered).
- You can erase unwanted characters, of those typed in so far during this insertion, by pressing BACKSPACE once for each character.
- You are able to erase all the characters typed so far on any whole line, after the first RETURN is typed during the insertion, by pressing the DEL key. The DEL key is sometimes marked as RUBOUT; see Appendix A or B for your terminal if it has neither key. Press the DEL key repeatedly to remove additional lines typed in during the current insertion.
- When you decide to keep the text typed in during the use of the "Insert:" world, press the ETX key for "end of text."
- If you decide to leave the "Insert:" world without keeping any of the characters already typed in, press the ESC key for "escape." See Appendix A or B for equivalent if there is no ESC key on your keyboard. This will terminate the "Insert:" world, and return you to the "Edit:" world, with the displayed text again just as it was before you entered the insertion.

Try using the DEL and ESC keys while using the I(nsert command to observe what happens.

3.3.2 The D(elete Command

I continue now from the point where you have THEREE on the screen following the use of I(nsert. To obtain THERE, you will have to *delete* the last E (or the one before it). Move the cursor to point to the E you wish to remove.

Press D, for D(elete, and observe that the screen now displays what is shown in display 3.5.

```
)Delete: ( ) (Moving commands) ((etx) to delete, (esc) to abort)
PROGRAM STRING1;
BEGIN
   WRITE('HI');
   WRITE(' ','THERE');
   WRITELN; (* Moves to start of next line *)
   WRITE('HI THERE');
   WRITELN(' THISA DEMSTATION');
   WRITELN('OF PROGRAM EXECUTION)
END.
```

Display 3.5: The prompt line shown upon entering "Delete:" world form the "Edit:" world using the command D for D)elete.

Caution: On some computer terminals the ESC key is located right next to the BACKSPACE key or the RETURN key. On such keyboards, one must be careful to avoid accidental depression of the ESC key, especially when long segments of text are being input.

To delete one or more characters, move the cursor to the right, or to following lines, using the regular cursor moving commands. Each character deleted disappears off the screen. For example, you can delete "E"); by pressing the right-arrow four times. Just as with the "Insert:" world, you can back up by using the BACKSPACE key. However, in the "Delete:" world, you *restore* characters to the screen when you use the BACKSPACE.

Finally, when you are ready to terminate the deletion, press ETX. This will return you to the "Edit:" world, with the text redisplayed and the deleted characters eliminated. You can terminate the deletion using ESC, just as you can ESC out of the "Insert:" world. Again, the displayed text returns to the status it had before you entered the D(elete world.

3.3.3 Finish Fixing the Other Errors

Now try your hand with the Editor by fixing the errors on the last two lines in display 3.4 containing "WRITELN." The next to last line contains spelling errors. The last line lacks an apostrophe just before the ")".

3.3.4 Q(uit and U(pdate your Workfile

At this point, you should be ready to compile and test the small program displayed on your screen. Press Q for Q(uit, and you will be shown a selection of three or four options, as shown in display 3.6.

Press U (for U(pdate) to cause the Pascal program you have been working on to be saved in your workfile on the disk. If you press E, the Editor will terminate and return to the "Command:" world, *without saving anything you have done with the Editor!* Press R to R(eturn back into the "Edit:" world. The R(eturn option saves you from embarrassing problems if you press Q(uit by mistake while in the "Edit:" world. After selecting U(pdate, you will hear some clicking of the disk while your program text is saved in the Workfile, and then you will be back in the "Command:" world. (The W(rite command, if available, is useful to record a copy of your text without leaving the Editor.)

```
>Quit:
      U(pdate the workfile and leave
      E(xit without updating
      R(eturn to the editor without updating
      W(rite to a file name and return
█
```

Display 3.6: Options for Q(uit command of the "Edit:" world. The normal choice is to U)pdate a file after you edit it. But if you have made a mistake during your editing you can completely ignore all effects of the editing session by E(xiting without saving the file. You can R(eturn to the editor if you did not really intend to leave. And, you can W(rite the edited file out to a named file instead of the current work file.

3.3.5 R(un your Program (If Possible)

Now press R for R(un (from the "Command:" world). The result should be a notice at the top of the screen saying:

    Compiling . . .

followed by much clicking and some additional displayed information. I will defer explaining what is happening here until Chapter 6. For now, these displayed lines tell you that the Compiler is busy trying to translate your Pascal program in the workfile into the *code* form that can be executed by the computer. If the Compiler finds no errors, it will save the executable code form of your workfile on the disk, and then will cause your program to start executing (ie: to start running). You will be notified that this is happening by the legend "Running . . . " at the top of the screen.

3.3.6 Coping with a Compile-time Syntax Error

If the Compiler does find an error in your Pascal program, it will not be able to save the code form of your workfile on the disk, nor will it start execution of your program. Instead, after more clicking of the disk you will find yourself presented with a message and an opportunity to either continue the compilation or to go back in the "Edit:" world. If you decide to continue the compilation by pressing RETURN, then you may find that some later error messages are spurious, caused by the first error. But, by continuing the compilation, especially with a printer and a long program containing few errors, you can take notes about what to fix when you later enter the editor.

If you answer the compiler's query about continuing the compilation by entering an E, you will enter the editor with the cursor pointing automatically at the *end of the logical item* where the Compiler found the error. (If your copy of the UCSD Pascal System has been preset for "student" use, this action occurs automatically.) A message displayed in the prompt line will give an explanation of the error the Compiler found. An error found by the Compiler is called a syntax error because it indicates that you have violated one or more of the formal syntax rules which describe how a Pascal program should be constructed. See Chapter 6, Pascal Compiler–Coping with Program Errors, for more details on this point. Press the SPACEBAR to display the "Edit:" world's prompt line so that you can fix the problem.

> *These comments about return to the editor from a compilation refer to the operation of the standard Screen-Oriented Editor of the UCSD Pascal System. As you become more familiar with the system and need to edit programs or text files which will not fit in memory all at once, you may want to use the large file editor, which comes on the UCSD Pascal System diskettes with the name "L2.CODE." This L2 editor understands all the commands of the standard Screen-Oriented Editor, although on leaving the editor the "W" option is not available, it has a few additional commands which enable you to manipulate files larger than the memory available in your computer. For documentation, see the main system reference manual for the UCSD Pascal System.*
>
> *When using the L2 editor as the system editor by changing its name from L2.CODE to SYSTEM.EDITOR with the Filer, the automatic placement of the cursor at the precise spot of a compilation error does not occur. This restriction applies to versions of the L2 editor available at the time of publication of this book.*

3.4 Saving your Workfile in the Disk Directory

Eventually, you will finish editing and testing revised versions of your program. You may then wish to start working on a completely different program, but may also wish to save the completed program so that it can be used again at a later time. To do this, use the F (for F(ile) command when in the "Com-

```
Filer: G(et, S(ave, W(hat, N(ew, L(dir, R(en, C(hng, T(rans, D(ate, Q(uit [A ▌
```

Display 3.7: The prompt line just after entering the Filer.

mand:" world. After some clicking of the disk, you should receive the display shown in display 3.7. The prompt line may contain only the initial letters of these commands if your screen is narrower than 80 columns.

3.4.1 First Check your Disk Directory Using L(ist

Press L (for L(ist) to see the list of titles of all the files currently stored on your disk. The L(ist command requests data input whereby you tell it which disk to refer to. In the UCSD Pascal System, each disk has a *volume identifier*, which is the name of the disk. This allows you to use two or more disks even on a machine that has only one disk drive. For the present example, respond to the prompt requesting a volume identifier by pressing ":" (the colon key) followed by RETURN. The Filer will respond by listing the directory showing your disk's contents. Display 3.8 shows approximately the directory listing you should receive at this point.

The number of entries with names prefixed by "SYSTEM." will differ depending upon whether your beginner's version of the UCSD Pascal System uses one or two diskettes. Note the two directory entries labelled SYSTEM.WRK.TEXT and SYSTEM.WRK.CODE. These are the two files associated with your workfile. The first is the form saved by the Editor when

```
Filer: G(et, S(ave, W(hat, N(ew, L(dir, R(en, C(hng, T(rans, D(ate, Q(uit [F.5]
DEMO:
SYSTEM.FILER      32   8-Jan-79
SYSTEM.COMPILER   69   8-Jan-79
SYSTEM.PASCAL     38   8-Jan-79
SYSTEM.EDITOR     45   8-Jan-79
SYSTEM.PDP-11     21   8-Jan-79
SYSTEM.CHARSET     5  29-Jan-78
SYSTEM.LINKER     21   8-Jan-79
SYSTEM.SYNTAX     14   8-Jan-79
SYSTEM.LIBRARY    17   1-Jan-79
STRING61.TEXT      4   8-Jan-79
GRAPH1.TEXT        4   8-Jan-79
GRAPH1.CODE        2   8-Jan-79
TURTLE.CODE       10   1-Jan-79
QUIZ1.CODE        45   8-Jan-79
ORIENTER.CODE     12   3-Nov-78
EDITDEMO.TEXT      4  14-Dec-78
COMPDEMO.TEXT      6  26-Dec-78
STRING61.CODE      2   6-Apr-79
SYSTEM.WRK.TEXT    4   7-May-79
SYSTEM.WRK.CODE    2   7-May-79
20/20 files(listed/in-dir), 357 blocks used, 127 unused
```

Display 3.8: Response to the Filer's L(ist Command.

you use Q(uit followed by U(pdate starting in the "Edit:" world. The second is the executable form of the same Pascal program, which was saved on the disk by the Compiler.

3.4.2 Now S(ave the Workfile

Press S (for S(ave) and note the prompt for a file title on the line just below the top line. If the workfile has not yet been S(aved in a previous version, you will receive the message shown in display 3.9. You type in a name followed by RETURN to complete the S(ave command. If you do not wish to lose a

```
Save as what file ? 
```

Display 3.9: S(ave command's prompt when the workfile has not previously been saved.

```
Filer: G(et, S(ave, W(hat, N(ew, L(dir, R(en, C(hng, T(rans, D(ate, Q(uit [F.5]
DEMO:
SYSTEM.FILER       32    8-Jan-79
SYSTEM.COMPILER    69    8-Jan-79
SYSTEM.PASCAL      38    8-Jan-79
SYSTEM.EDITOR      45    8-Jan-79
SYSTEM.PDP-11      21    8-Jan-79
SYSTEM.CHARSET      5   29-Jan-78
SYSTEM.LINKER      21    8-Jan-79
SYSTEM.SYNTAX      14    8-Jan-79
SYSTEM.LIBRARY     17    1-Jan-79
STRING1.TEXT        4    8-Jan-79
GRAPH1.TEXT         4    8-Jan-79
GRAPH1.CODE         2    8-Jan-79
TURTLE.CODE        10    1-Jan-79
QUIZ1.CODE         45    8-Jan-79
ORIENTER.CODE      12    3-Nov-78
EDITDEMO.TEXT       4   14-Dec-78
COMPDEMO.TEXT       6   26-Dec-78
STRING1.CODE        2    6-Apr-79
NEWNAME.TEXT        4    7-May-79
NEWNAME.CODE        2    7-May-79
20/20 files(listed/in-dir), 357 blocks used, 127 unused
```

Display 3.10: Listing of directory after S(ave of "NEWNAME".

```
Save as NEWNAME ?
```

Display 3.11: S(ave command's prompt if file of the same name is already on the disk.

previously S(aved workfile, use a name different from any other already in use in the disk's directory. Suppose you respond to the prompt by typing in "NEWNAME" followed by RETURN. Now repeat the L(ist command to see the result, which is shown in display 3.10.

Notice that the entries which had been shown as SYSTEM.WRK.TEXT and SYSTEM.WRK.CODE are now shown as NEWNAME.TEXT and NEWNAME.CODE, respectively. If the Filer had found a previously saved file of the same name, it would respond with a different prompt for the S(ave command, as shown in display 3.11. You can respond to this prompt either with Y (for Y(es) or N (for N(o). If yes, then the previously saved files called NEWNAME.TEXT and NEWNAME.CODE will be removed from the disk directory, and your new version of the workfile(s) will be given the names:

NEWNAME.TEXT
NEWNAME.CODE

If you respond to the prompt with no, the Filer will prompt with:

Save as what file?

as described above, and you can then use almost any new name not already in use in the disk directory. Note, however, that a workfile name cannot be longer than 10 characters (plus ".CODE" or ".TEXT").

3.4.3 What to Do if You Want to Change a Previously Saved Workfile

You often will save a workfile only to realize that you need to make changes in that workfile at a later time. The Filer's G(et command allows you to designate the name of an old file as the current name associated with the workfile. Press G (for G(et) and note the prompt message that appears in response. If the response is:

Get what file?

then you can type in any name previously entered when S(ave was used in connection with a workfile (that still is stored on your disk). If it finds the directory entry for the file name you give it, the Filer will respond with:

Text and Code files loaded

or:

Text file loaded

or:

Code file loaded

as the case may be. If the Filer prompts with:

Throw away current workfile?

you have the opportunity to avoid possible loss of your files named SYSTEM.WRK.TEXT and SYSTEM.WRK.CODE by typing N (for N(o). If you type Y (for Y(es) the Filer will discard your old unsaved workfile, and then prompt you for the file name you want loaded as your new workfile as described above.

If you change your mind after starting the G(et command, you can return back to the "File:" world by pressing the ESC key, or by typing in the name of a nonexistent file followed by RETURN. After using G(et to establish the name of a previously saved file as the current workfile, you can leave the "File:" world using Q(uit. This returns you to the "Command:" world. If you then use E(dit, the Editor's world will be entered, and the first screen-full of the now current workfile will be displayed. If you use C(ompile, instead of E(dit, the Compiler will proceed to try to translate the form of your now current workfile into executable form. If the Compiler succeeds, it will save the resulting executable file, as usual, as SYSTEM.WRK.CODE. Regardless of whether the Compiler succeeds, use of the Compiler will cause any previous file with the directory name of SYSTEM.WRK.CODE to be removed from the directory.

If, upon reaching the "Command:" world after leaving the "File:" world, you use the R(un command, the system will attempt to execute the currently saved form of your workfile without using either the Compiler or the Editor. If there is no code form of the workfile on the disk, the Compiler will be invoked to translate the text form of the workfile into executable form.

3.5 Suppress Execution of the Maze at Bootload Time

When you first receive the UCSD Pascal System, the "Maze:" world may always appear immediately after you bootload the system. As soon as you feel familiar with the idea of single character commands, you will probably want to dispense with the "Maze:" and "Date:" world exercises. To do this, enter the "File:" world by using the F(ile command while in the "Command:" world.

Now use the L(ist command, as described earlier in this chapter, and note the entry called SYSTEM.STARTUP. That entry is a special *reserved* name used with the code form of a program workfile called ORIENTER. The ORIENTER workfile contains the programs that create both the "Maze:" and "Data:" worlds. You can retain that file, but suppress its automatic execution at bootload time, by changing its name back to ORIENTER.CODE. To do this, press C (for C(hange). The Filer will prompt with:

Change what file?

You answer by typing in:

SYSTEM.STARTUP

followed by RETURN. The Filer will respond with:

Change to what?

You answer by typing in:

ORIENTER.CODE

followed by RETURN.

If you have followed these steps without error, the final result will be indicated by a message verifying that the change has been made. Having made that change, you should no longer have a file called SYSTEM.STARTUP on your disk. You might want to check to make sure that this is correct by using the Filer's L(ist command.

It may help to explain what we have been doing here. When you bootload the System, it is programmed to look through the disk directory for an executable file called SYSTEM.STARTUP. If one is present, the program contained in that file is loaded into memory and executed automatically. If no such file is present on the disk, then bootloading takes you immediately to the "Command:" world. Now, try bootloading again to verify that this indeed is what happens.

You may wish to get rid of the file containing the "Maze:" and "Data:" worlds entirely, in order to release space on your disk for other uses. To do this, see Chapter 5, File Manager, regarding the R(emove command.

4 Screen Editor

4.1 Goals for this Chapter

To use the UCSD Pascal System effectively, you need to be familiar enough with the Screen Editor to use it as a convenient tool. The main goal of this chapter is to provide you with a reference summary of how the Editor is used. In each section, the order of presentation starts with the Editor's facilities you are likely to use most often. See Appendix C.1 for an alphabetic summary of the Editor's commands with references to descriptive text in this chapter.

Many beginners do not bother to learn how to use all the available facilities of the Editor. While you can make extensive use of the UCSD Pascal System by knowing how to use only a small part of the Editor's facilities, it will probably save time to become familiar with each of the Editor's commands.

Specific goals for this chapter include the following:

- Learn to use each of the principal commands of the Editor to the point where you are comfortable in using them as tools.
- Edit a file established as the current workfile by the Filer, one named at the time when the Editor starts up, and a new file not previously stored on the disk.
- Terminate the Editor by updating the current workfile, by exiting without update, and by writing a named file to disk. Check using the Filer to see what happens in each case.

4.2 Editor Overview

The Editor is the UCSD Pascal System's principal tool for creating, reading, and changing text files, ie: files of information in the form directly readable by humans when displayed. There are two versions of the Screen Editor. The version provided as a standard part of the System is designed to work with the entire contents of a text file in the computer's main memory as one unit. A large file version of the Screen Editor is also available as part of the advanced version of the System. Even on a machine with only 48 K bytes of memory (and no part of the UCSD Pascal System in read-only memory) the beginner's version of the Screen Editor can usually handle more than 250 lines of Pascal program text in one file. The Compiler provides a convenient means for combining several of these files into a single large program, so that there is minimal need to use the advanced large file version of the Screen Editor.

Since your display screen cannot display the entire contents of most workfiles, the screen is used as a movable *window* through which you can view the contents of the workfile. You point at the place in the workfile you wish to view by moving the cursor up or down with the commands provided. When moving the cursor has the effect of shifting to a text line not currently displayed on the screen, the Editor automatically moves the window so as to display the section of text to which the cursor has been moved. In addition to various commands provided to *move* the cursor form place to place in the workfile, there are also commands with which you can *change* the content of the workfile at the place where the cursor points.

The simplest of the *cursor movement* commands are the up-pointing and down-pointing arrows (or their equivalents described for your keyboard in Appendix A or B), and the arrow keys pointing right and left. Though the content of the Editor's window is displayed as a sequence of lines as in a page of printed text, you can think of the workfile stored in the computer's memory as if it were stored on one, long, thin, continuous strip of paper, with all the lines connected end to end. Therefore, when the cursor is at the right end of one displayed line, pressing the right arrow once moves the cursor to the left end of the next line below on the display. Similarly, when the cursor points to the left-most nonblank character in a line, pressing the left arrow returns you to the right end of the line above.

In addition to the four arrow command keys, there are several other commands for *moving* the cursor. If you know of a word or other string of characters stored in the workfile, you can use the F(ind command to scan through the workfile to look for that word or string rapidly. You can also S(et *markers* in the workfile and use the J(ump command to shift the displayed window to any one of the markers. Markers at the B(eginning and E(nd of the workfile are built into the Editor and you do not need to use the S(et command to establish their positions. There is also a P(age command which allows you to shift the displayed window one screen-full at a time. The direction of the shift depends on whether the *direction* flag in the upper left corner of the screen points right (">"), ie: toward the end of the workfile, or left ("<"), ie: toward the beginning.

Press the keys containing the brackets ">" and "<" to change the pointing direction. Press the TAB key, if your keyboard has one, to shift the cursor eight columns to the right or left in the workfile, depending on which direction the flag indicates. Press the RETURN key to command the cursor to move to the left-most character of the line following the line where the cursor currently points. Type a number before any of these commands to cause the command to be repeated any number of times. The number will not be echoed on your screen as you type.

Most of the other commands of the Editor are used to *change* the contents of the workfile. I(nsert allows you to type text into the workfile starting at the position immediately before the character pointed at by the cursor when you enter the I(nsert command's world. D(elete allows you to remove characters from the workfile, beginning where the cursor points when you enter the D(elete: world, and ending where the cursor points when you press ETX (or equivalent on your keyboard). R(eplace is an extension of the F(ind comand. This allows you to specify a string of characters to substitute for the word or string which is found after scanning through the workfile. C(opy is used to insert into the workfile a passage of text that has previously been saved temporarily in a buffer area of the computer's memory following an I(nsert or D(elete command. C(opy can also be used to insert a portion of the text stored in another named workfile. The A(djust command allows you to shift the entire line where the cursor is currently located to the left or to the right. The eX(change command lets you type over characters stored in the workfile on a one-for-one basis. Therefore the steps needed to make changes in the text are simplified.

When you finish editing a workfile and need to move on to other activities, use the Editor's Q(uit comand. This command offers several options. The U(pdate option causes the text stored in the computer's memory to be saved on the disk under the reserved workfile name SYSTEM.WRK.TEXT. *Any previous version of your workfile will be lost when this happens!* The E(xit option allows you to leave the Editor without changing anything on the disk. In this case, the text stored in the computer's memory is lost! The W(rite option allows saving the text stored in the computer's memory under a name that you can designate. This option permits you to continue editing without having to restart the Editor. (W(rite is not available in the large file ["L2"] editor.) The R(eturn option is provided to allow you to continue editing even if you trigger the Q(uit command by pressing Q inadvertently.

4.3 Cursor Movement Commands

To provide an example large enough to give you worthwhile practice with the Editor, I will use the workfile EDITDEMO, which is supplied in one of the disk files associated with your copy of the system. This workfile contains a Pascal program which combines the programs REPEAT1 and REPEAT2, which are presented in Chapter 3 Section 8 of the book *Microcomputer Problem Solving Using Pascal*, referred to in Chapter 1 of this book. Each of these two programs has been changed into a procedure in order to produce a

workfile long enough to occupy at least two windows when viewed on a
24-line display screen. The program contained in the EDITDEMO workfile can
be compiled and executed, but it is supplied to you primarily for use as a
starter file for practicing with the Editor.

*Note that the text of the two programs (procedures) has been altered
slightly from that printed in the Bowles textbook. This has been done to
keep all lines of text within the boundaries of a display which is 40 columns
wide. Most microcomputer displays offer 64 or 80 columns screen width.
We restrict the presentation here to 40 columns because that is the screen
width available on the popular Apple II computer. If you are using an
Apple II, or another machine with only 40 columns screen width, see the
sections of Appendices A and B regarding your machine for notes on how to
simulate a screen 80 columns wide using the UCSD Pascal System.*

To get started, enter the Filer from the "Command:" world by pressing F.
Then use the G(et command to establish EDITDEMO as your current
workfile. Next Q(uit from the Filer, and press E (for E(dit) from the "Command:" world. The result should be as shown in display 4.1.

```
)Edit: A(djst C(py D(lete F(ind I(nsrt J(mp R(place Q(uit X(chng Z(ap  [E.6f]
PROGRAM EDITDEMO;

PROCEDURE REPEAT1;
VAR S,SG:STRING;
    L,N:INTEGER;
BEGIN
  WRITELN(
    'TYPE ANY STRING FOLLOWED BY <RET>'
        );
  READLN(S);
  N:=1;
  L:=LENGTH(S);
  REPEAT
    SG:=COPY(S,1,N);
    WRITELN(SG);
    N:=N+1;
  UNTIL N>L
END (*REPEAT1*);

PROCEDURE REPEAT2;
VAR S:STRING;

PROCEDURE REVERSE;
```

Display 4.1: The display on entry to the Editor with the EDITDEMO workfile.

4.3.1 Arrow Commands and their Relatives

Many machines used with the UCSD Pascal System have keyboards which
include four arrow keys intended for moving the cursor around on the screen.
The up arrow moves the cursor up one line on the screen, the down arrow one
line down. The right and left pointing arrow keys similarly move the cursor
one position to the right or left. If your keyboard lacks any of these keys, see

the appropriate sections of Appendices A and B for instructions on how to simulate the actions of these keys on your keyboard. If you want a more detailed introduction to the use of the cursor positioning arrow keys, see the sections of Chapter 2 which present the Maze example.

As an exercise at this point, note a specific place in the displayed text of the EDITDEMO program. Move the cursor to that place using the arrow keys. Notice that movement to the right or left will only place the cursor within the group of characters starting with the left-most non blank character on a line, and ending with the blank following the right-most non blank character. This is intended to be a convenience to users, since the long runs of blank characters displayed elsewhere on the screen are not actually stored in the computer's memory. Vertical movement through the runs of blanks is permitted however. For example, start with the cursor pointing at the "G" in "STRING" within the long line just 2 lines below "BEGIN" in the REPEAT1 procedure, then press the down arrow 6 times to reach ";" in the line:

    SG: = COPY(S, 1, N);

Now press the up arrow once, leaving the cursor in the line just above the ";". Next press the left arrow once, and note that the cursor jumps to the "T" in "REPEAT".

4.3.2 Repeated Execution of an Arrow Command

On many keyboards, there is a facility automatically allowing you to simulate repeated pressing of some keys, often including the arrow keys. This is sometimes accomplished by holding down the key to be repeated for about one-half second or more. On other keyboards, there is an auxiliary REPEAT key which must be pressed in conjunction with the key you want to be repeated. If your keyboard has this facility, try using it along with the arrow keys for easier movement of the cursor. If your keyboard lacks the repetition feature, the Editor program provides a partial substitute. To see how it works, place the cursor again on the "G" in "STRING" in the line:

    'TYPE ANY STRING FOLLOWED BY <RET>'

within the REPEAT 1 procedure. Now press the "6" key followed by the down arrow. The cursor should again jump to the ";" in:

    SG: = COPY(S, 1, N);

You can cause repeated execution of many Editor commands by first typing in the number of repetitions you want.

4.3.3 Moving the Cursor Off the Screen

Try moving the cursor to the bottom line of the screen. Now press the down arrow, and note that the entire content of the screen shifts *up* one line. This is equivalent to moving the displayed window *down* in the text by one line, thus revealing an additional line at the bottom of the screen, and hiding a line at the top. Continue pressing the down arrow until the line:

PROCEDURE REPEAT2;

appears on the top line of the screen. On a 24-line screen, the effect should be as shown in display 4.2.

```
PROCEDURE REPEAT2;
VAR S:STRING;

PROCEDURE REVERSE;
  (*REVERSE THE ORDER OF CHARACTERS
     IN S*)
VAR NB,NE:INTEGER;
    (*BEGIN AND END POINTERS*)
    SAVE:CHAR;
BEGIN
  NB:=1;
  NE:=LENGTH(S);
  REPEAT
    (*EXCHANGE CHAR'S NB & NE,
       SHIFT NB & NE *)
    SAVE:=S[NE];
    S[NE]:=S[NB];
    S[NB]:=SAVE;
    NB:=NB+1;
    NE:=NE-1;
  UNTIL NB=NE;
END (*REVERSE*);

BEGIN (*REPEAT2*)
```

Display 4.2: *The display of EDITDEMO following multiple uses of the down arrow key.*

The upward shifting of the screen contents is called *scrolling*, as if the displayed text were actually on a scroll of paper being pulled upwards behind the screen's window. You cause the screen content to scroll upwards by one line with the Editor, if the cursor is located in the bottom line of the screen and you press the down arrow. This keeps the cursor within the displayed window. Continue pressing the down arrow (or use the repeat feature) causing the text to scroll upwards until it stops scrolling. The cursor will then be in the last line of text in the workfile, presenting the display shown in display 4.3.

Shifting the cursor off-screen in the other direction is more awkward on most machines because they lack facilities for scrolling downwards. To see what happens, move the cursor upwards carefully until it rests in the top line displayed on the screen. Now press the up arrow one more time. The result should be as shown in display 4.4.

In this situation as in several others, the Editor solves the problem of displaying the new cursor position by clearing the screen and then re-displaying to show a window with the cursor in the middle line of the screen. On slower terminals, this operation can take considerable time.

```
BEGIN (*REPEAT2*)
  WRITELN(
    'TYPE ANY STRING FOLLOWED BY <RET>'
      );
  READLN(S);
  WHILE LENGTH(S)>0 DO
  BEGIN
    REVERSE;
    WRITELN(S);
    WRITELN;
    WRITELN('TYPE ANOTHER STRING');
    READLN(S);
  END;
END (*REPEAT2*);

BEGIN (*MAIN PROGRAM*)
  WRITELN('START EDITDEMO');
  WRITELN;
  REPEAT1;
  WRITELN;
  REPEAT2;
END
```

Display 4.3: The display of EDITDEMO after scrolling to the end of the workfile.

```
>Edit: A(djst C(py D(lete F(ind I(nsrt J(mp R(place Q(uit X(chng Z(ap  [E.6f]
  NE:=LENGTH(S);
  REPEAT
    (*EXCHANGE CHAR'S NB & NE,
      SHIFT NB & NE *)
    SAVE:=S[NE];
    S[NE]:=S[NB];
    S[NB]:=SAVE;
    NB:=NB+1;
    NE:=NE-1;
  UNTIL NB=NE;
  END (*REVERSE*);

BEGIN (*REPEAT2*)
  WRITELN(
    'TYPE ANY STRING FOLLOWED BY <RET>'
      );
  READLN(S);
  WHILE LENGTH(S)>0 DO
  BEGIN
    REVERSE;
    WRITELN(S);
    WRITELN;
    WRITELN('TYPE ANOTHER STRING');
```

Display 4.4: The display following the use of the up arrow in the top line.

4.3.4 Using SPACE, BACKSPACE, and RETURN

The SPACE bar can be used to substitute for both the right arrow and the left arrow when you are in the "Edit:" or "Delete:" world. When the Editor's

direction flag, located in the upper left corner of the screen, points forward
(">") the SPACE bar substitutes for the right arrow. When the direction flag
points backwards ("<"), ie: toward the beginning of the workfile, the SPACE
bar substitutes for the left arrow.

The BACKSPACE key is equivalent to the left arrow when you are in the
"Edit:" or "Delete:" world. The Editor's direction flag has no effect on the
operation of the BACKSPACE key. On some keyboards which do not have a
BACKSPACE key, the combination CTRL/H has the same effect. See Appendix A or B for your machine.

The RETURN key causes the cursor to jump to the beginning of the next
line. If the Editor's direction flag points forward, then the RETURN key moves
the cursor to the first nonblank character on the next lower line in the
workfile. The displayed window is scrolled upwards if necessary to display the
next line. If the Editor's direction flag points backwards, then the RETURN
key moves the cursor to the first nonblank character on the previous line in the
workfile. The screen window is redisplayed if the RETURN key is pressed
when the cursor is located in the top line of text on the screen and when that
line is not the first line in the workfile.

You might wonder why no special provision has been made to cause the cursor to jump easily to the *end* of the next or previous line in the workfile. This
can be done by the simple expedient of jumping to the beginning of the line
following the line whose end you wish to jump to. Then press the
BACKSPACE (or left arrow) key once.

4.3.5 The TAB Key

The TAB key is used as an express version of the SPACE key in the Editor.
Each time you press TAB, the cursor is moved until it coincides with a column
at which a new group of eight columns starts. Thus the TAB stops are located
at columns 1, 9, 17, 25, 33, ...If the Editor's return flag points forward,
then the TAB moves the cursor toward the end of the workfile. If necessary it
jumps from the end of one line to the beginning of the next. If the flag points
backwards, then the TAB moves the cursor towards the beginning of the
workfile. In some versions of the Editor, it will be possible to change the positions of the TAB-stop columns. At the time this book is being written, that
feature is not ready to be released to users.

4.3.6 The P(age Command

The P(age command is an express equivalent of the up arrow and down
arrow commands of the "Edit:" world. It is similar in concept to the TAB key
command, but moves the cursor whole lines up or down in the workfile
depending upon the current status of the Editor's direction flag. If the direction
flag points forward, then the P(age command causes the display *and the cursor*
to move forward in the workfile as many lines as the screen window is high.
Thus, if the screen is 24 lines high, the displayed window will show the next 24
lines in the workfile. The cursor's position *on the screen* will remain the same,
but its logical position will be moved forward by 24 lines. Similarly, if the

direction flag points backwards then the P(age command will jump to the previous group of screen-height lines. At the end of the workfile, the P(age command may not display a complete window full if there are not enough additional lines available in the workfile to fill the screen. In that case, the cursor will be placed at the end of the file, and only the top half of the window will be filled.

4.3.7 The J(ump Command and Its Relatives

The Editor's J(ump command provides a means by which to move the cursor quickly from one place in the file to another without having to use the up or down arrow commands repeatedly. Here is the prompt line displayed by the J(ump command:

>JUMP: B(eginning E(nd M(arker <esc>

Respond to this prompt with B(eginning, and the cursor will be moved suddenly to the beginning of the workfile. Similarly, E(nd places the cursor at the end of the workfile. In both cases, the screen window will be redisplayed if necessary. If you respond with M(arker, the Editor will respond with the following prompt:

Jump to what marker?

This refers to markers that you can place anywhere in the workfile using the S(et command. As used with many commands in the Editor, you can press the ESC key to simply terminate the J(ump command's world without doing anything.

4.3.8 The S(et Command Used for Setting Markers

The S(et command has several different purposes. These are mainly related to setting *switches* which control how the Editor operates. It can also be used to read the current values of those switches. For purposes of this section on cursor movement commands, we will only be concerned with setting markers into the workfile for use with the J(ump command. Various other switches that can be reached with the S(et command are intended mainly for use in word processing applications and are discussed later in this chapter.

To establish a marker, use the S(et command when in the "Edit:" world. The result will be the prompt line:

>Set: E(nvironment M(arker <esc>

If you respond with M(arker, the Editor's prompt will be:

Set what marker?

to which you can respond with a number, name, or other short identifier terminated by RETURN. The position of the marker will be the position of the cursor at the time you enter the S(et command.

As an example go through the sequence of steps needed to display the portion of the EDITDEMO file shown in display 4.4. Place the cursor in the blank line between "END (*REVERSE*);" and "BEGIN. . ." which is two lines below. Now use S(et to establish a marker simply called "1." (Do not type in the quotes when responding to the command.) You can check to see the result of doing this by using the E(nvironment option of the S(et command. The response from this option should be as shown in display 4.5 if you have successfully established a marker called "1." You can terminate the E(nvironment option and the S(et command by pressing SPACE.

```
)Environment: (options) <etx> or <sp> to leave█
    A(uto indent   True
    F(illing       False
    L(eft margin   0
    R(ight margin  79
    P(ara margin   5
    C(ommand ch    t
    T(oken def     True

    968 bytes used, 15928 available.

    Markers:
        1

    Date Created: 12-14-78   Last Used: 12-14-78
```

Display 4.5: In the "Edit:" world. Here is the S(et command's environment with marker 1 established.

4.3.9 J(umping to Markers

Now use J(ump to move the cursor to the B(eginning of the workfile. The result should be as shown in display 4.1. Next, J(ump to the E(nd of the workfile, getting something like display 4.3. In this case, the cursor will be at the very last character position in the workfile, rather than at the beginning of the last line, as resulted from the sequence of steps that led to display 4.3.

Neither of the displays reached by jumping to the beginning or the end of the workfile shows the text which includes the marker "1" which was set in the previous subsection. Now use J(ump, respond to the prompt with M(arker, and then with "1" followed by RETURN. The Editor will respond with a display like that shown in display 4.4, and with the cursor at the same position it had when you established the marker.

You can establish only a limited number of markers in a workfile, usually 10 in current versions of the UCSD Pascal System. The Editor will keep track of the logical position of each marker, even when you change the contents of the workfile. Of course, if you delete a section of text containing a marker, it does not make sense to maintain the position of the marker. In this case, the position of the marker may show up almost anywhere in the text that remains. If you use more than two or three markers, it will generally be difficult to remember their logical positions in the text unless you give them names that suggest their locations. However, the Editor will remember only the first 8 characters of a long marker name. If you want to reuse a marker name at a new location, simply set it again. If you try to set too many different markers, the Editor will prompt you on steps to follow in replacing one of the markers already established. You can always get a listing of the markers currently established (but not their locations) by using the E(nvironment option of the S(et command.

4.3.10 The F(ind Command

Often you will want to jump to a position in a workfile where you have not previously thought to leave a marker. If you remember a small part of the contents of the text near that place, you can easily get there using the F(ind command. To see how the F(ind command works, using the EDITDEMO file as an example, jump to the beginning of the workfile (again leading to the display 4.1). Now press F to enter the F(ind command's world, with the prompt line:

>Find[1]: L(it <target> =>

The Editor now waits for you to type in a pattern string of characters which will be the *target* of a fast search through the workfile. Before proceeding further, make sure that the Editor's direction flag points forward, as shown in the prompt line above. If it does not, press ESC, change the direction flag by pressing ">", and again enter the F(ind command.

As an example, respond to the prompt shown above by typing in:

/BEGIN/

The two characters "/" serve to bracket or *delimit* the string of characters which are to be found in the workfile, and they are not included in the target. You can use any special character as a delimiter, including either the single or double quote symbols. We use the right slash (/) because it is conveniently located on the keyboard, and it rarely is included in the target of a F(ind command.

Note that the F(ind command distinguishes between uppercase and lowercase characters. If you typed in "begin" or "Begin" rather than "BEGIN," the command will respond by telling you that it could not find any occurrence of the target string.

As soon as you press the delimiter key ("/" in this example) for the second time, the F(ind command will start searching through the workfile looking for an occurrence matching the target string you have typed in. If all goes well in our example, the F(ind command will complete its work and the cursor will be left pointing at the end of the sixth line of the workfile's text, immediately *following* the target pattern "BEGIN." If at any time, while typing in your desired target string, you decide that you wish to terminate the F(ind command so as to start over again, just press the ESC (escape) key.

4.3.11 Multiple Occurrences of the Target

In many cases, you will pick a target string that occurs more than once in the workfile. The F(ind command starts searching (in the direction shown by the Editor's direction flag) from the current position of the cursor. After F(inding the first occurrence of the target, the cursor will be displayed immediately following that target. You may well be looking for a later re-occurrence of the same target. It is simple enough to repeat the same F(ind comand at this point, again typing in the same target string. However, there is an easier way.

Continuing our example with the target "BEGIN", again press F to enter the F(ind command. Now simply press the S key (for S(ame), and note what happens. The cursor will jump to the end of the next occurrence of "BEGIN" in the workfile. Keep doing this several times, noting what happens. Once the last occurrence of "BEGIN" has been found in the workfile, an error message will appear in the prompt line at the top of the screen. In further uses of the F(ind command using the same target, the Editor will refuse to move the cursor any further.

Now jump back to the beginning of the workfile. This time, press 2 before pressing F to enter the F(ind command. Note that the F(ind command's prompt now appears as follows:

> Find[2]: L(it < target > = > __

with the digit "2" appearing within the square brackets. This is the F(ind command's *repeat factor*, showing how many times the search for the target string will be repeated once typing of the target has been completed. You can type in any whole number as a repeat factor before typing F. This feature is not designed to make it convenient to type in large repeat factors, and the value of the repeat factor will not be shown on the screen until the F(ind command's own prompt line is displayed. You can get the result of using a very large repeat factor without having to think about its value by typing "/" as a repeat factor. Upon entering F(ind the resulting prompt will be:

> Find["/"]: L(it < target > = > __

The result of doing this should be to find the *last occurrence* of the target within the Workfile.

4.3.12 Finding Backwards

As mentioned earlier, the F(ind command conducts its search in the direction shown by the Editor's direction flag. So far we have been finding items only in the forward direction. Now jump to the end of the workfile, and then set the direction flag to backwards by pressing the "<" key. Next, use F(ind for the S(ame target, noticing that the cursor stops at the *end* of the last occurrence of "BEGIN." Use F(ind followed by S(ame again (without repeat factor) and note that the cursor does not move. This is because the search starts from the current cursor position, and, of course, the first occurrence of the target found in the backwards direction is the one already adjacent to the cursor's position.

To perform a multiple search in the backwards direction, you may find any of several tactics useful. After stopping at one occurrence of the target, you can get to the next previous occurrence by using a repeat factor of 2. Another possibility is to use the up arrow once, thus placing the cursor in the line above the one where an occurrence of the target has just been found. This has the effect of putting the cursor at a position in the workfile preceding the target's occurence just found, and another application of F(ind followed by S(ame will no longer encounter that occurrence. Just as one can use the infinite repeat factor [/] to find the last occurrence of the target when going forward, you can use the same repeat factor when going backwards to find the *first* occurrence of the target starting from the end of the workfile.

4.3.13 L(iteral Targets vs Tokens

Unless you use the L(it option of the F(ind command (before typing in the first delimiter of your target) the Editor will assume that you want to locate a <target> consisting of one or more *tokens*. A token may be a complete word, a number, a special (punctuation) character, or an *identifier*. In many programming languages as in Pascal, an identifier is defined as a string of characters which must start with a letter, and thereafter may consist of additional letters or digits. For example,

```
A
abc
n123
X25p
```

are all identifiers in this context. In the F(ind command, the Editor distinguishes between uppercase and lowercase letters, regardless of the rules on this subject for any programming language. Thus:

```
BEGIN
begin
Begin
beGIn
```

are regarded as four different <target>s.

The F(ind command permits you to string together several different tokens into a single <target>. Moreover, it is indifferent to the number of blank space characters between tokens in the workfile. For example, a <target> typed in as:

    S:STRING;

would be matched in the Workfile by any of the following:

    S:STRING;
    S : STRING ;
    S: STRING;
    S: STRING;

or even:

    S:
    STRING;

In the last of these examples, the <target> appears in pieces shown on two successive lines. For the purposes of the F(ind command, the end-of-line marker separating two successive lines is to be regarded as equivalent to one blank character. This is equivalent to the definition of end-of-line marks in a file of type text in Pascal.

To understand the distinction between a token and a literal <target>, jump back to the beginning of the EDITDEMO Workfile. Enter the F(ind command and use the <target>:

    /PROC/

noting that the Editor will claim that this target cannot be found. This is because the <target> typed in does not match any complete token in the workfile. Now enter F(ind again, this time pressing the L key followed by the S key. The cursor will come to rest pointing at the character E within the first occurrence of "PROCEDURE". The L(iteral option of the F(ind comand tells the Editor to look for a <target> string which *exactly matches* the <target> that you type in. In the L(iteral option, blank characters count exactly as they are found, and all of the <target> string examples shown in the group just above will be regarded as different.

4.3.14 The "=" Key Command

After finding a <target> that you want, it may sometimes be more convenient to have the cursor placed where the <target> begins rather than at its end. Press the "=" key, when this situation is desired, and the cursor will be moved to the beginning of the <target>. In fact, the "=' key command serves as an equivalent of a jump to beginning of the "target" key even after you have used several other cursor movement commands following the F(ind.

(However, the destination of the "=" key command will change to the beginning of the most recent insertion if you use the I(nsert command.)

4.3.15 The V(erify Command

The V(erify command is used to redisplay the contents of the Editor's window, placing the cursor as near to the center of the screen as is sensible. Occasionally, the Editor will lose track of characters displayed on the screen which should have been moved. If you have any doubt about the correctness of the displayed text following any command that changes the content of the workfile, use the V(erify command to get a fresh display. The window displayed by the V(erify command will be a correct representation of the text stored in the computer's memory.

4.4 Commands which Change the Workfile's Contents

All of the commands described in this section are designed for use in changing the contents of the workfile copy currently stored in the computer's main memory. All of the commands described in the previous section are used for moving the cursor from place to place in the workfile, but they do not change the contents of the workfile. Some of the commands described in this section are designed so that you can change your mind after altering the workfile contents, and can return to the status of the workfile as it was before the command was entered.

Remember that the changes you make using the commands described in this section affect only the copy of the workfile in the computer's active memory. They have no affect on any copies stored on a disk. Changes on the disk are only made through the Q(uit command which is described in the next major section of this chapter. In general, it is a good idea to save the results of your editing changes in the workfile on the disk periodically, (eg: once every ten minutes or so). If instead you work without saving the workfile for a long period, you leave yourself vulnerable to losing all your work during that period if the electric power should fail. Since the main memory of most microcomputers retains its stored information only as long as the electric power is maintained, even a momentary failure of power could result in the loss of your work. If you save your work every ten minutes or so, you will only lose a few minutes worth of work in case of a power failure.

4.4.1 I(nsert

The I(nsert command puts the Editor in a mode allowing you to type information into the workfile. All text characters typed while in the "I(nsert:" world become part of the workfile stored in main memory, if you terminate the I(nsert using the ETX (End of Text) key. On some keyboards the ETX key must be simulated, usually with the combination of the CONTROL (or CTRL) and C keys (see Appendix A or B for details regarding your machine). If, after inserting a substantial amount of text, you decide to back up and start over again, the ESC key allows termination of the I(nsert command without saving anything typed, since the command was last entered. On some keyboards,

ESC must be simulated, usually with the combination CTRL/X (again see Appendix A or B for details).

The entry of information typed while in the "I(nsert:" world starts at the position where the cursor points when the I(nsert command is entered. As noted in the previous section, the cursor's logical position can never be to the left of the left-most nonblank character on a line, nor to the right of the position immediately following the right-most nonblank character on a line. If the cursor's position is between those two limits when you enter the I(nsert command, the Editor will split the characters already on the same line. The portion starting at the cursor's position, when I(nsert is entered, will be pushed as far as possible to the right side of the screen. This is illustrated in display 4.6 using a screen capable of displaying a full 80 characters of text. If your screen is not as wide, the Editor will only push the right portion of the line as far as possible within the actual width of the screen. (UCSD Pascal for the Apple II

```
>Insert: Text (<bs> a char,<del> a line) [<etx> accepts, <esc> escapes]
PROGRAM EDITDEMO;

PROCEDURE REPEAT1;
VAR S,SG:STRING;
    L,N:INTEGER;
BEGIN
  WRITELN(
    'TYPE ANY STRI█                              NG FOLLOWED BY <RET>'
    );
  READLN(S);
  N:=1;
  L:=LENGTH(S);
  REPEAT
    SG:=COPY(S,1,N);
    WRITELN(SG);
    N:=N+1;
  UNTIL N>L
END (*REPEAT1*);

PROCEDURE REPEAT2;
VAR S:STRING;

PROCEDURE REVERSE;
```

Display 4.6: A display of the screen after beginning the I(nsert command with the cursor in the middle of a line. Note how the characters to the right of the cursor have been pushed as far as possible to the right.

Computer is supplied to regard the screen logically 80-columns wide, but actually displaying only 40 columns at any window.)

Now if you type characters into the gap within the split line, the display will remain stable unless you type enough characters to fill up the gap. Display 4.7 shows what occurs when you type in more characters than will fit within the gap.

Notice that the right side of the line where the cursor started remains on the screen, but it has been moved down one line to make room for additional text to be entered. Notice also that when this happens, all the subsequent lines in the workfile are removed from the screen. This should be of no concern to you. These subsequent lines of text are still stored in the computer's memory. They have been removed from the screen simply to make room for you to type in as many lines of additional text as you like.

To continue typing at the beginning of the next line below, press the RETURN key. Notice that the result of doing this is to place the cursor immediately below the left-most character on the line from which the RETURN key was pressed. Display 4.8 shows the result of typing in "XX" immediately after pressing RETURN following the state of the workfile shown in display 4.7.

```
)Insert: Text (<bs> a char,<del> a line) [<etx> accepts, <esc> escapes]
PROGRAM EDITDEMO;

PROCEDURE REPEAT1;
VAR S,SG:STRING;
    L,N:INTEGER;
BEGIN
  WRITELN(
    'TYPE ANY STRIxyzxyzxyzxyzxyzxyzxyzxyzxyzxyzxyzxyzxyzxyz█
                                              NG FOLLOWED BY <RET>'
```

Display 4.7: Starting with the situation as shown in display 4.6, here we have entered a long series of "xyz" characters. After the gap in the original line is filled in with new characters, the remainder of the original line is moved down and the balance of the screen below is cleared.

In some cases you may not wish the indentation of a new line to be the same as that of the line from which RETURN is pressed. You can change the indentation if you press either SPACE or BACKSPACE *immediately following a RETURN* and before typing in any other text. Once you have typed in any character other than a space or a backspace at the beginning of the line, use of SPACE or BACKSPACE on that line will no longer affect the indentation.

Quite often you will make errors while typing in characters. If you have not typed in too many characters following an error, the easiest remedy is to use BACKSPACE to remove the offending characters from the screen. Each time you press BACKSPACE while in the "I(nsert:" world, one character previously typed-in will disappear from the screen. Naturally, after all characters typed in during the present I(nsert command have been removed, no additional characters that were previously there will be removed. You can use the D(elete command to dispose of characters displayed when in the "Edit:" world.

The DEL key (for delete; sometimes labeled RUBOUT) can be used when in the I(nsert command's world as an express version of the BACKSPACE key. Each time DEL is pressed, you remove the entire line where the cursor is located, and the cursor returns to the end of the previous line. The DEL key cannot be used to remove the line where the cursor was located when I(nsert was entered, and an error message will appear on the prompt line if you try to do this.

Occasionally, you may have reason to type in enough characters on one line to cause part of the line to be displayed beyond the right limit of the screen, if that were possible. If you do this, the editor will notify you of the problem by displaying an exclamation point (!) at the right margin of the screen. The portion of the text that cannot be displayed on that line is still stored in the computer's memory. To have it displayed again on the screen, you may wish to split the line into two by inserting a RETURN in the middle of the line. Another possibility is to shift the whole line to the left, resulting in a smaller indentation. This can be done with the A(djust command, which is explained in a later section.

A common inadvertent error is the attempt to type in nonvisible control characters, like the cursor positioning arrows. The result of doing this will be the display of question mark characters. You can erase these characters in the usual manner, as with any other errors.

```
)Insert: Text (<bs> a char,<del> a line) [<etx> accepts, <esc> escapes]
PROGRAM EDITDEMO;

PROCEDURE REPEAT1;
VAR S,SG:STRING;
    L,N:INTEGER;
BEGIN
  WRITELN(
    'TYPE ANY STRIxyzxyzxyzxyzxyzxyzxyzxyzxyzxyzxyzxyzxyzxyz
    xx█
                                            NG FOLLOWED BY <RET>'
```

Display 4.8: Continuing the insertion of display 4.7, with a RETURN followed by "xx".

4.4.2 D(elete

The D(elete command is used to remove characters from the text stored in the workfile copy in the computer's memory. After entering the D(elete command, you can move the cursor using any of the cursor-moving comands described in Section 4.3.1 of this chapter, ie: the arrow commands and their relatives. J(ump and F(ind do not work within the D(elete command's world.

We can refer to the position of the cursor, when the D(elete command is entered, as the *entry position*. Upon moving the cursor to another position, note that all the characters between the new position and the entry position are erased from the screen. As an example, consider the first window displayed for the EDITDEMO workfile, as shown in display 4.1. Place the cursor so that it points at the "R" in "REPEAT" in the third line of the program. Enter D(elete, then press the down arrow twice. The result should be as shown in display 4.9. Now press the BACKSPACE key several times noting that characters backed over in this fashion reappear on the screen.

As with the I(nsert command, you can terminate the D(elete command in either of two ways. Press ETX to complete the job of removing the text enclosed between the entry position and final position of the cursor, as established during use of D(elete. Press ESC to terminate D(elete in such a way as to leave the workfile just as it was before the D(elete was entered.

```
>Delete: ( ) (Moving conmmands) ((etx) to delete, (esc) to abort)
PROGRAM EDITDEMO;

PROCEDURE

          EGER;
BEGIN
  WRITELN(
     'TYPE ANY STRING FOLLOWED BY <RET>'
          );
  READLN(S);
  N:=1;
  L:=LENGTH(S);
  REPEAT
     SG:=COPY(S,1,N);
     WRITELN(SG);
     N:=N+1;
  UNTIL N>L
END (*REPEAT1*);

PROCEDURE REPEAT2;
VAR S:STRING;

PROCEDURE REVERSE;
```

Display 4.9: An example of the D(elete command after pressing the down arrow twice.

4.4.3 R(eplace

The R(eplace command is an extension of the F(ind command. For details on the F(ind command, see Section 4.3.3. Upon entering the R(eplace command, the following prompt line is displayed:

>Replace[1]: L(it V(fy <targ> <sub> =>

The bracketed number and "L(it" have the same meaning as they do with the F(ind command. "<targ>" is an abbreviated reference to the same <target> as used with F(ind. As in the F(ind command, after typing the <target> explicitly once, subsequent uses of the same <target> can be made by using S for S(ame. In fact, you can use F(ind to establish the <target>, and then use the S(ame option with R(eplace to refer to the same <target>. Similarly, you can establish the <target> explicitly using R(eplace, and then use F(ind with the S(ame option to refer to the same <target>. After R(eplace carries out the same search as accomplished by F(ind, it deletes the found occurrence of the <target> and then inserts the substitution string indicated by "<sub>". As an example, you might respond to the prompt shown above by typing in:

   /BEGIN//START/

with the result that the first occurrence of "BEGIN" will be changed to "START." Although both <target> and substitution strings are of the same length in this case, they need not be of equal lengths. In fact the substitution string can be of zero length, with the result that the <target> string will simply be deleted from the workfile after it is found. As with the F(ind command, you can use a repeat factor with R(eplace. Use the slash repeat factor (/) to change all occurrences of the <target> to the substitution string.

   Often you will want to change *some* occurrences of the <target> string but not all of them in the workfile. You can change the occurrences that are found by R(eplace selectively by using the V(erify option (abbreviated "V(fy" to keep the prompt line as short as possible.) The V must be included in your response to the "R(eplace" prompt *before* you type in the substitution string. A convenient way to go through most of your workfile with R(eplace, selectively changing only some occurrences of the <target>, is to use the slash repeat factor (/) along with the V(erify option. Each time a new occurrence of the <target> is found, the following prompt will appear:

   >Replace[/]: <esc> aborts, 'R' replaces, ' ' doesn't

You then have three options: press R to complete the replacement of that occurrence with the <substitution> string, and to cause the cursor to move on to the next occurrence of the <target>; press the SPACE bar to bypass the substitution, but allow the search to continue for the next occurrence of the <target>; or press ESC to cause the R(eplace command to be terminated at that point without either making the substitution or continuing the search.

4.4.4 C(opy

   The C(opy command is used to insert passages of text that have previously been saved in the workfile at the cursor's position. The C(opy command's prompt is as follows:

   Copy: B(uffer F(rom file <esc>

showing that the command has two distinct options.

The B(uffer option is used together with a passage of text that is automatically saved in a buffer area of the computer's memory whenever you use either the I(nsert or the D(elete command. Each use of I(nsert or D(elete saves the associated passage of text in the buffer area, *removing the previously saved contents of the buffer*. After entering C(opy, press B (for B(uffer) to have a copy of the buffer's saved contents inserted in the workfile at the place where the cursor points.

It is important to note that the buffer is filled with a new passage of text whether you terminate the I(nsert or D(elete using either ETX or ESC. Thus is it possible to mark a passage of text within the workfile using the D(elete for later copying, but to leave the original passage intact by terminating the D(elete using ESC.

As an example of the use of the B(uffer option, jump to the beginning of the EDITDEMO workfile, then carry out the following steps (the display should be the same as shown in display 4.1). First, move the cursor to point to the "V" in "VAR" on the fourth line of the display. Now enter D(elete and press RETURN twice. The result will be to blank out the two lines:

```
VAR S,SG:STRING;
    L,N:INTEGER;
```

from the display. Next, press ESC, with the result that the display will again appear as in display 4.1. Now move the cursor up two lines, so that it points at the left end of the blank line between "PROGRAM . . ." and "PROCEDURE . . .". Next, press C for C(opy followed by B for B(uffer. The result should be as shown in display 4.10. Note that the original two lines following 'PRO-CEDURE . . ." still remain in the display. They could have been eliminated in the same operation by terminating the D(elete command using ETX as usual.

The F(rom file option of the C(opy command is used in a similar manner, but draws its passage of text from another workfile saved on the disk. If you use this option, the Editor will prompt you to type the name of the file to be copied into the current workfile. You can copy just a portion of another workfile starting at one marker and continuing to a second marker saved in that workfile. Those markers must be established using the Editor while working with the other workfile. It is not possible to set markers in the other workfile without using Q(uit to get out of the Editor, typically updating the current workfile as you go. The prompt line for the F(rom file option is as follows:

> Copy: From what file[marker,marker]?

The pair of marker names can be omitted, and the result will be that the entire file whose name is typed will be copied. Enclose two marker names within square brackets. This will produce only that portion of the named workfile enclosed between the two markers copied into the current workfile. Of course, the first marker should be placed earlier than the second marker in the other workfile to make this operation sensible.

4.4.5 A(djust

The A(djust command is used to shift selected lines of text to the right or left without changing their contents. Either single lines or groups of lines can be

```
)Edit: A(djst C(py D(lete F(ind I(nsrt J(np R(place Q(uit X(chng Z(ap  [E.6f]
PROGRAM EDITDEMO;
▌AR S,SG:STRING;
    L,N:INTEGER;

PROCEDURE REPEAT1;
VAR S,SG:STRING;
    L,N:INTEGER;
BEGIN
  WRITELN(
    'TYPE ANY STRING FOLLOWED BY <RET>'
        );
  READLN(S);
  N:=1;
  L:=LENGTH(S);
  REPEAT
    SG:=COPY(S,1,N);
    WRITELN(SG);
    N:=N+1;
  UNTIL N>L
END (*REPEAT1*);

PROCEDURE REPEAT2;
VAR S:STRING;
```

Display 4.10: The display of EDITDEMO looks like this after using the C(opy command to copy two lines from the B(uffer.

shifted. The A(djust command has several options shown in its prompt line as follows:

> Adjust: L(just R(just C(enter <left, right, up, down arrows> <etx>

All of the options refer to the line in which the cursor is located. L(just causes that line to be left justified, ie: to be pushed to the left as far as possible. R(just causes the cursor's line to be pushed as far right as specified by the right margin currently specified for the Editor. To find at which columns the right and left margins are currently set, use the E(nvironment option of the S(et command. C(enter causes the cursor's line to be placed half-way between the left and right margins as currently specified.

The left and right arrows cause the cursor's line to be shifted one position in the indicated direction each time they are pressed. If you want to shift a group of lines the same number of positions, start with the top line of the group and shift it the desired amount using the left and/or right arrow keys. Next, press the down arrow once for each additional line that you want shifted. A similar strategy applies by first shifting the bottom line of the group, then using the up arrow for the other lines of the group. The best way to see how this works is to experiment with it.

You terminate the A(djust command using the ETX key or its equivalent. There are no means provided whereby you can use ESC to escape out of the A(djust command in a way that will restore the text to the status it had before the A(djust command was entered.

4.4.6 eX(change

Sometimes it is necessary to change a few characters in the workfile on a one-for-one basis. The eX(change command allows you to simply type over characters already in the workfile without going through the complications of using D(elete followed by I(nsert. Press "X" to enter the eX(change command. Display 4.11 exemplifies how the eX(change command is used.

```
)eXchange: TEXT ((bs) a char) [(esc) escapes; (etx) accepts]
PROGRAM EDITDEMO;

PROCEDURE REPEAT1;
VAR S,SG:STRING;
    L,N:INTEGER;
BEGIN
  WRITELN(
    'type any str▉NG FOLLOWED BY (RET)'
      );
  READLN(S);
  N:=1;
  L:=LENGTH(S);
  REPEAT
    SG:=COPY(S,1,N);
    WRITELN(SG);
    N:=N+1;
  UNTIL N>L
END (*REPEAT1*);

PROCEDURE REPEAT2;
VAR S STRING;

PROCEDURE REVERSE;
```

Display 4.11: An illustration of the eX(change command.

To reproduce this example, jump to the beginning of the EDITDEMO workfile as in display 4.1. Move the cursor to point at the "T" at the left end of the long line beginning " TYPE ANY . . . .!". Now enter eX(change by typing "X". Next, type "type any str". If your keyboard does not have lowercase characters, any alternative string will do just as well.

Each character typed replaces one that had been in the workfile when the eX(change command was entered. Use BACKSPACE to wipe out one of the newly typed characters, restoring the original character to the screen. When you have no further characters to exchange, press ETX to make the changes permanent. Press ESC to cancel any changes made so far by the eX(change command, and to restore the text of the workfile to the status it had before the eX(change command was entered.

4.4.7 Z(ap

The Z(ap command is designed to be used following F(ind, R(eplace, and

I(nsert commands. *[Caution: do not try to use Z(ap if you follow any one of these three commands with any other command that changes the text of the workfile, or any command that moves the cursor — the results will be hard to predict.]* If the most recent text changing command was I(nsert, Z(ap deletes the text that was inserted. Thus, if you end an insertion using ETX, and then realize that you made a mistake, Z(ap allows you to start over again. If the most recent command was F(ind, then Z(ap deletes the occurrence of the < target > string that was found. If the most recent command was R)eplace, then Z(ap deletes the substitution string from the text of the workfile.

Following Z(ap, you can use the B)uffer option of the C(opy command to restore the text that was deleted by Z(ap. Thus Z(ap provides an "express" method for finding a < target > and then moving it to an alternate place within the workfile. You use F(ind, followed by Z(ap, then move the cursor to an alternate location, and finally use C(opy followed by B(uffer.

If you use a repeat factor with either F(ind or R(eplace, only the most recent < target > or substitution string will be deleted by the Z(ap command. If you repeat the Z(ap command, it will delete the contents of the C(opy buffer, with the effect that C(opy cannot be used to restore the effect of the first Z(ap of the group. After Z(ap has been used once, repetition will have no effect on the stored text in the workfile, until you use F(ind, R(eplace, or I(nsert again.

4.5 The Q(uit Command and its Options

The Q(uit command is used to leave the Editor in an orderly manner. Use of the Q(uit command is required if you wish to save the results of an editing session in which you have changed your workfile. You could also terminate an editing session in a more drastic way by bootloading again, or by withdrawing your disk from the machine. The prompt messages that appear for the Q(uit command were shown in display 3.6.

The U(pdate option causes the contents of the computer's memory to be saved on the disk in the reserved file SYSTEM.WRK.TEXT, ie: in the "unnamed" workfile on the disk. Any previously saved file called SYSTEM.WRK.TEXT will be removed from the disk as a result of this action. Having reached the Q(uit command, there is no way for you to change the name of the file SYSTEM.WRK.TEXT. This is already saved on the disk, in order to prevent it from being removed. However, you can use the W(rite option of the Q(uit command to save the contents of the computer's memory resulting from the current Editor session, under a different file name. You can then use the E(xit option to prevent the old version of the workfile from being removed from the disk.

The E(xit option terminates the Editor without taking any action at all to save the contents of the computer's memory. You might use the E(xit option after using the Editor to *read* the contents of a workfile without making any changes. E(xit from the Editor will then have no affect on your disk directory. Since data errors can sometimes be caused in the process of reading information from the disk, or writing to it, it is best to avoid any more disk operations than necessary. The E(xit option is a facility designed to assist in avoiding disk operations that are not needed.

The R(eturn option is provided for those of us who develop sloppy habits in typing into the Editor. If you hit the "Q" key inadvertently, you may not have it in mind to terminate the Editor session quite yet. Press "R" (for R(eturn) to get back into the Editor at the same place you had been before the Q(uit was invoked.

The W(rite option allows you to save the current contents of the computer's memory in a named disk file. After the disk file has been saved, the Editor session continues. The W(rite option requests a file name using the following prompt:

Name of output file (<cr> to return) -->

You can respond by typing in the name you want the workfile to be saved under (leaving out ".TEXT") and following with RETURN. If you simply press the RETURN key (referred to here as <cr> for carriage return), no disk file will be saved and the Q(uit command will be terminated as if you had used the R(eturn option. If you do respond to the W(rite option with a file name, the Editor will notify you when the disk file has been saved, and then will offer you the option of exiting or returning to the Editor. The W)rite option is especially useful if your current system disk is so full that there is insufficient space in which to store the newly edited text. Insert an alternate disk (which has been initialized with a UCSD Pascal System directory) and use the volume name of that disk (or "#4:") as part of the new file name. Example #4: NEWTEXT.

4.6 Using the Editor for Word Processing

The principal difference between uses of the Editor for word processing and for editing programs, is the automatic *filling* of each line of a paragraph. In filling, the Editor scans ahead for the right margin, keeping track of the beginning of the last word you typed in. If the Editor detects that the current word you are typing would extend past the right margin, it automatically moves the current word to the beginning of the next line, *"filling"* in the rest of the previous line with blanks. To prepare the Editor for paragraph filling, you will need to use the S(et command to change several switches in the Editor's environment. (A switch is an option which has only two states, such as "Yes" or "No," "True" or "False.") Display 4.5 shows roughly the display you should get using the E(nvironment option of the S(et command when the Editor is first entered.

As an exercise to see how paragraph filling works, change the A(uto indent option to false, and the F(illing option to true. If your screen is not a full 80 columns wide, also change the R(ight margin to a smaller value. For example, on the Apple II computer you might want to change the R(ight margin to 39.

Within the E(nvironment sub-command's world, you select an option to be changed by typing its leading character. For example, to change the F(illing option type "F". The Editor responds by placing the cursor at the first character position of the current value of the option, eg: over the "F" in "False." The legend "False" will simultaneously disappear. Now type T, and observe that the displayed value of the option changes to "True." Similarly, to change the A(uto indent option, type A followed by F (for "False") or T (for "True").

Now you can type in a small paragraph. Notice that you do not need to use the RETURN key to get from the end of one line to the beginning of the next. If the last word you attempt to type into a line cannot fit within the established margins, the Editor will move the word to the beginning of the next line. With a small paragraph on the screen, now try an insertion in the middle of that paragraph. The Editor will refill all of the lines following the point of the insertion, putting as many words as possible within each line, adjusting the lines so that the last word of each line does not extend past the right margin, or is not split between two lines.

Deleting a portion of a paragraph is slightly more complicated. To see how it works, delete several words from the middle of your paragraph. After completing the deletion (with ETX), notice that the lines within your paragraph have not been refilled to give the appearance of a properly filled paragraph. Instead, you have to call for the filling explicitly by using the M(argin command in the "Edit:" world. After pressing M to initiate the M(argin command, the screen will go blank for several seconds. The paragraph will then be redisplayed with all lines correctly filled.

Within the Editor's environment switches, the L(eft margin and R(ight margin have the obvious roles of limiting the left and right extent of a paragraph. The P(ara margin (for "Paragraph margin") switch refers to the indentation of the first line of a paragraph. If you want to change the appearance of any single paragraph, use the following steps:

- S(et the E(nvironment switches to the desired values (and leave the S(et command by pressing SPACE).
- Place the cursor at any point within the paragraph to be changed.
- Press M for M(argin.

For word processing, the Editor is designed to be used in conjunction with a formatter program. The formatter takes a text file as input, and sends the output to a printer or to another file. In addition to the edited text , the formatted output contains page numbers, headings, and footings, and suitable margins at top and bottom of the printed page. The formatter may also be used to adjust the blank spaces on each line of a paragraph so as to make both right and left margins show a regular appearance. A preliminary version of a formatter for the UCSD Pascal System has been in use for some time, and was used in printing the Bowles textbook cited in Chapter 1 of this book. A good general-purpose formatter has been long delayed, but is nearing completion for general distribution as this book is going to press. For readers familiar with the UNIX (trademark of Bell Laboratories) operating system, the new UCSD Pascal formatter will have a command structure similar to that of NROFF, the UNIX formatter.

In general, the formatter program requires a small number of commands to be embedded in the edited text. The usual practice is to place an escape character in the left-most column of a line, thus identifying the line as containing a command rather than text. The formatter then interprets the marked line as a command, and does not attempt to print the content of that line. For editing purposes, the command line has the same appearance as any other line of text. The escape character normally used in the UCSD Pascal Editor is the upward arrow (↑). Another character often used for the same purpose is the period (.). You can use the E(nvironment option of the S(et command to change the command escape character to be used by the formatter to any desired character.

For purposes of the M(argin command, the Editor recognizes the beginning and ending lines of a paragraph by looking for either of the following:

- a completely blank line,
- a line beginning with the formatter's command character.

No attempt is made to include a command line within the filled part of a paragraph.

As a final note on word processing uses of the Editor, do not try using the M(argin command when the cursor is within a table of data, or in some other passage which you do not want to be filled as if it were a paragraph. The Editor will prevent this from happening if F(illing is set false. If you inadvertently work on a Pascal program with F(illing set true, and if margin is also inadvertently used the results become unreadable.

5 File Manager (Filer)

5.1 Goals for this Chapter

The File Manager which is called the "Filer," is the UCSD Pascal System's principal tool for keeping track of files stored on your disks. The main goal of this chapter is to provide you with a reference summary of how the Filer is used. As in Chapter 4, the order of presentation starts with the facilities you are most likely to use frequently. See Appendix C2 for an alphabetic summary of the Filer's commands, with references to descriptions in this chapter.

The full set of facilities provided with the Filer is extensive, and goes beyond the range of tasks many beginners will need to handle. Following is a list of specific learning goals for beginners. A good grasp of each of these goals will simplify the use of the UCSD Pascal System considerably.

- Establish a previously saved file as the current Workfile for use with the Editor and Compiler.
- Save the current Workfile in the disk directory for later use.
- Create a new clean Workfile without destroying any previous Workfile.
- Remove unwanted old files from your disk directory. Eliminate scattered empty areas on the disk if necessary to make room for new files.
- Transfer a file, or group of files, from one disk to another. Transfer a text file to your console display device or to a remote terminal or printer.
- Establish the current directory date of your disk.

- Initialize a new or used disk by clearing it of any previous contents using the Z(ero command.
- Change the directory title of an old file so that you can reuse the same title for a new file without losing the old file.
- Check your disk for possible bad blocks. Use "eX(amine" to attempt a repair of low quality areas of the disk.
- Use the "wild card" file title characters '=' and '?' to simplify the use of certain commands applied to whole groups of files.

5.2 Overview of Files and the Filer

A point of confusion for novice users of the UCSD Pascal System is that the term *file* has several related but distinct meanings. Within a Pascal program, an identifier declared to be of a type associated with a file provides a means of referring to an input/output device. We will call this identifier the file's *internal identifier*. The device may be a video display, a keyboard, a disk drive, a remote terminal, a printer, or any one of many other possible items of peripheral equipment.

If the input/output (I/O) device is a disk drive or perhaps a tape drive, it is used for storing and retrieving information recorded on a secondary storage medium such as a floppy disk. In this case, there is usually room for storage of many different collections of information, each separately referred to as a file. A typical file on the disk might be all the Pascal program statements for a single program, or the executable code version or another program, or possibly a collection of data designed to be used by another program. To keep track of all the stored files, a *directory* of the files is stored on the disk. Each disk has its own directory, which is available to the System only when the disk is actually mounted in a disk drive connected to the computer. The directory is basically a listing of the names of the files on the disk, their locations, the amount of space they occupy, and other items of importance to the System.

5.2.1 Volume Identifiers

To distinguish between separate disks, each disk is given a *volume identifier*, ie: a name for the disk which is also stored in the directory. The volume identifier should begin with a letter, and may consist of a total of 7 letters and digits. The full *external identifier* of a disk file consists of the volume identifier followed by the directory name of the file. In order that the System may distinguish between the volume identifier and the directory name, the two are separated by a colon (:). For example, you might have a disk with a volume identifier of CLASS, and on that disk a file with a directory name of TESTPROG.TEXT. The full title of the file would therefore be CLASS.TESTPROG.TEXT.

Volume identifiers in the UCSD Pascal System refer not only to disks but also to peripheral devices which have no directories. For example, the principal CRT (or teleprinter) terminal of a small computer has the volume identifier "CONSOLE:". Since that device has no directory and is not subdivided logically into files, "CONSOLE:" is its full title, with no characters to the right of the colon. Your machine may also have facilities to handle the predeclared volumes:

PRINTER:
REMOUT:
REMIN:

where "REMOUT:" and "REMIN:" are used for communicating with a remote terminal device or telephone line. You can get a listing of the volumes currently available on your machine by using the Filer's V(olumes command.

5.2.2 Simplified Titles for Disk Files

The UCSD Pascal System allows the user to refer to a disk file in several different ways. For example, this can be accomplished either by typing in a response to a prompt, or by executing a Pascal program statement that refers to the file. In certain common circumstances, the reference can be made without specifying the volume identifier explicitly.

If a reference to a file title lacks a volume identifier entirely, the System assumes that the volume intended is the *default volume*. When you bootload, the disk volume containing the UCSD Pascal operating system (the file SYSTEM.PASCAL) is initially considered to be the default volume. If the volume identifier of the disk from which you bootload is "MYDISK:" and you have a file called FIRSTPROG.TEXT on that disk, then that file can be referred to by either of the following title strings:

MYDISK:FIRSTPROG.TEXT
FIRSTPROG.TEXT

with the same results. You can use the Filer's P(refix command to change the default volume identifier to some disk other than the one from which you bootloaded. Then it will still be possible to refer to the same file on "MYDISK:" by either of the following:

MYDISK:FIRSTPROG.TEXT
*FIRSTPROG.TEXT

where the '*' is interpreted by the System as a substitute for the bootload disk's volume identifier. These conventions are designed to reduce the amount of typing you need to do to refer to files on several different disks, particularly when using the Filer.

5.2.3 Naming Conventions to Simplify Work with Groups of Files

Since you will often have to work with a disk that has dozens of directory entries, it sometimes becomes desirable to perform similar operations on many directory entries all at once. The Filer provides several naming conventions that simplify these operations. One common tactic is to construct the directory titles of all files belonging to a related group of files using the same prefix. For example, most of the files provided to you as part of the system software of the UCSD Pascal System are identified by the prefix "SYSTEM," and include the files:

SYSTEM.COMPILER
SYSTEM.PASCAL
SYSTEM.EDITOR
SYSTEM.FILER

The period (.) is included to make the file titles more readable to humans, and has no special significance to the System. Because some users of the System are accustomed to using other separator characters for this purpose, you can also use the characters '/', '\', '-', and '__' in file directory titles.

Some of the Filer's commands permit selective reference to all files which have the same prefix or suffix. If one of these commands prompts for a file title, and you respond with:

SYSTEM=

the command would refer to all of the files in the list shown above. The character '=' is a *wild card* which substitutes for any characters in a title following the prefix "SYSTEM". In the list of files shown above:

SYS=

or

SYSTEM.=

would have equivalent results. If you have a mixture of files with ".TEXT" and ".CODE" suffixes, the generalized title:

=.TEXT

or

=TEXT

would refer only to the ".TEXT" files and not to the ".CODE" files.

As an extension of the wild card concept, the Filer allows you to substitute the question mark (?) for the equals sign (=). The Filer will then halt upon reaching each directory entry associated with the prefix or suffix, and ask whether you wish the command to apply to that particular entry. You respond with 'Y' (for Y(es) if you wish the command to apply, and with any other character if not. The Filer will then continue searching through the directory looking for additional titles matching the wild card specification.

If you leave out the prefix *and* suffix in a file title, using only the '=' or '?' character, the Filer will refer to each title in the directory.

Another possibility is to "sandwich" the wild card character between prefix and suffix, as in:

PREF=SUFF

or

MINE?TEXT

The wild card naming conventions apply to the following commands: L(ist, E(xtended-directory, T(ransfer, R(emove, and C(hange.

5.3 Workfile Commands

The Workfile concept is designed to simplify the number of steps a user of the UCSD Pascal System has to take in editing, compiling and testing new programs. The Filer's Workfile commands are tools for handling the disk directory entries associated with the temporary "unnamed" Workfile and with saved Workfiles on the disk. Each Workfile may have a ".TEXT" part and a ".CODE" part. The ".TEXT" part is an independent disk file containing, in the case of computer programs, the Pascal or other source programming language statements of one program. The Text file is produced by the Editor as the result of an editing session. The ".CODE" part of a Workfile is another disk file containing executable code generated by the Compiler based on translation of the source language statements in a text file.

When you finish an Editor session, using the U(pdate option of the Q(uit command, the Editor leaves on disk a file called SYSTEM.WRK.TEXT, which is what we are calling the "unnamed" or temporary Workfile. The file title SYSTEM.WRK.TEXT is reserved by the System for this use. If you then use the "Command:" world's C(ompile command, the Compiler will be invoked, and it in turn will look for a file called SYSTEM.WRK.TEXT as its input. If the Compiler succeeds in translating the source language statements from the text file into executable code, it will leave on disk a file called SYSTEM.WRK.CODE. In the typical program development situation, you can then R(un the program from the "Command:" world's E(dit command, and the Editor automatically assumes that you want to work with the file SYSTEM.WRK.TEXT, if it is present on the disk.

As you can see, the two reserved file names, SYSTEM.WRK.TEXT and SYSTEM.WRK.CODE, provide a means of communication among the Editor, the Compiler, and the R(un command of the "Command:" world. When these files are present you do not need to respond to the E(dit, C(ompile, or R(un command with any file name, because it is assumed that you want to use the files with the reserved titles.

Of course you will eventually reach the stage where you want to save a version of the text and code files you have been working with in order to develop a different program. At that point, you enter the Filer, and use the S(ave command. The S(ave command asks for a name, which in practice can be up to 10 characters long. The Filer assumes that you want to retain the text and code suffixes in these file titles respectively, resulting in titles that are up to 15 characters long. You might respond to the S(ave command with the name PROBLEM1 followed by pressing the RETURN key, at which point the directory entry for SYSTEM.WRK.TEXT is changed to show its title as PROBLEM1.TEXT, and similarly the entry for SYSTEM.WRK.CODE is changed to PROBLEM1.CODE. The Filer now retains PROBLEM1 as the title of your current Workfile. You could verify this by using the Filer's W(hat command which displays the title of the current Workfile. At this point, the disk no longer contains any files called SYSTEM.WRK.TEXT or SYSTEM.WRK.CODE. However you could use Q(uit from the Filer, and use R(un in the "Command:" world, with the result that the System will start execution of the named Workfile, ie: PROBLEM1.CODE.

If you enter the Editor, using the "Command:" world's E(dit command, the Editor will load the contents of PROBLEM1.TEXT into the computer's memory in preparation for an Editing session. Subsequently, use of the U(pdate option of the Editor's Q(uit command will result in the creation of a new text file on disk called SYSTEM.WRK.TEXT. This file will be separate and independent of the file PROBLEM1.TEXT until or unless you return to the Filer and use the S(ave command. The S(ave command will then offer you the option of retaining the new temporary Workfile under the name PROBLEM1.TEXT. If you respond with Y(es, the old file under that same name will be removed from the disk, and the temporary Workfile will be given that name instead of SYSTEM.WRK.TEXT.

Of course many other scenarios are possible. You should find it helpful to experiment with the Filer's four Workfile commands to gain a better understanding of how the Workfile is used. Use the L(ist directory command, described in Section 4, to observe the directory changes that result from using the Workfile commands in conjunction with the Editor and Compiler.

5.3.1 G(et

Use the G(et command to establish an existing file (or a ".TEXT" and ".CODE" pair) as the current Workfile. If no files called SYSTEM.WRK.TEXT or SYSTEM.WRK.CODE are currently present in the disk directory, G(et will simply ask for the name of the Workfile you want loaded into memory. For example, your disk directory might include the files SNAP.TEXT and SNAP.CODE. When the filer responds to G(et with the prompt:

Get what file?

or just Get? to save space in computer memory. You might answer by typing:

SNAP

followed by RETURN. The Filer will respond with:

Text and Code file loaded

if it finds the Workfile, or:

No file loaded

if not. If SYSTEM.WRK.TEXT or SYSTEM.WRK.CODE already exists in the disk directory, then G(et will respond with:

Throw away current workfile?

If you answer with Y(es, then those files will be removed from the disk, and the System tables will be updated to show that the SNAP files are not to be regarded as the current Workfile. If you answer with anything other than Y(es, the G(et command will terminate with no effect, and the Filer's main prompt line will reappear. If you press G (for G(et) inadvertently, and wish to return to the main level of the Filer, answer the prompt simply by pressing RETURN.

5.3.2 S(ave

Once you have created a new temporary text Workfile with the Editor (ie: SYSTEM.WRK.TEXT) or a new temporary code Workfile with the Compiler (ie: SYSTEM.WRK.CODE) the S(ave command can be used to give those files permanent directory names. If the temporary files are actually on the disk, the S(ave command's prompt will be:

Save as what file?

or in some versions, Save as? to which you might answer:

WORK2

followed by RETURN. As a result, a directory entry for SYSTEM.WRK.TEXT will become WORK2.TEXT, and SYSTEM.WRK.CODE will become WORK2.CODE.

Please note: Any old files called WORK2.TEXT and WORK2.CODE will automatically be removed from the disk by this process and replaced with the new version of the Workfile. Thus, make sure you create a new name, or are not concerned with any older versions of the files of the same name.

5.3.3 N(ew

The N(ew command has the effect of clearing out the current Workfile recognized by the System so that you can begin creating a completely new text file with the Editor. If there is a SYSTEM.WRK.TEXT or SYSTEM.WRK.CODE on the disk when N(ew is entered, the Filer prompts with:

Throw away current workfile?

If you answer Y(es, then both the text and code files are removed from the disk. If you answer with any key other than Y, then the N(ew command is terminated without having any effect.

N(ew has no effect the actual disk files associated with a current workfile name. As in the examples presented in earlier subsections, you might have a named workfile SNAP active and associated with the disk files SNAP.TEXT and SNAP.CODE following use of the G(et command. You might then try to use N(ew, whether inadvetently or intentionally. Even if the temporary version(s) of the workfile in SYSTEM.WRK.TEXT and SYSTEM.WRK.CODE were thrown away by this process, the original files SNAP.TEXT and SNAP.CODE would not be touches by the N(ew command.

5.3.4 W(hat

The W(hat command is used to display the name of the currently active workfile. If the files SYSTEM.WRK.TEXT and/or SYSTEM.WRK.CODE are present, but no G(et operation has been done on a named Workfile, then the Filer will respond with:

workfile is not named (not saved)

If a G(et has been performed on a named workfile called SNAP, then the response to W(hat will be:

SNAP

If neither named or unnamed workfiles are present, then the response to W(hat will be:

No workfile

5.4 Status Checking/Setting Commands

The principal source of information about the status of files in the UCSD Pascal System is the directory of files stored on each disk. The contents of the directory can be displayed using the L(ist directory and E(xtended directory commands of the Filer.

The other commands in this group provide supplementary information on the V(olumes currently accessible to I/O operations, on the D(ate stored in the System disk from which you bootloaded, and on the default P(refix volume name currently in force.

5.4.1 L(ist Directory

The L(ist command normally is used to display part or all of the directory of a selected disk volume. The prompt to this command is

Dir listing of what vol?

or in some versions: Dir listing of?

You can answer with an abbreviated volume name, or a complete volume name. You can also provide an optional destination name requesting that the directory listing be sent to some device other than the principal console device of your machine. For example, the optional destination might be a printer connected to the "REMOUT:" I/O port.

To list the content of the System disk from which you have bootloaded, respond to the prompt by pressing the colon key (:) followed by RETURN. The resulting display will have roughly the appearance shown in display 5.1. If the directory is too long to be listed at once on the terminal screen, the Filer will stop after filling the screen. It will then prompt you to press the SPACE bar to continue, by displaying the next group of directory entries. If, at this point, you wish to terminate the L(ist command and leave the partial directory already on the screen, press the ESC key instead.

Sometimes you may have too long a directory to be listed all at once on the screen, but may wish to list only selected file titles from the entire directory. For example, you might wish to display only the titles of the text files on your disk. You can do this, when you respond to the L(ist command's prompt, by following the wild card naming conventions described in Section 5.2.3, as in:

=.TEXT

This will produce what is shown in display 5.2 which is based on the directory contents shown in display 5.1.

If you want to list the directory of a disk other than the one from which you bootloaded, then give its volume name. For example, to list all of the directory of a disk called OTHER, answer the L(ist command's prompt with:

OTHER:

followed by RETURN. If you want to list only the file titles prefixed by SYSTEM on that disk, answer with:

OTHER:SYSTEM=

followed by RETURN.

Sometimes it is useful to have a copy of the directory for one of your disks printed out on paper. If you have a teleprinter connected to the REMOUT: port of your computer, and wish to list out the directory of the disk called "SNAP:," then answer the L(ist command's prompt with:

OTHER:,REMOUT:

followed by RETURN.

5.4.2 V(olumes

The Volumes command will display a list of the identifiers of I/O volumes currently available to programs running on your machine. Display 5.3 shows

```
Filer: G(et, S(ave, W(hat, N(ew, L(dir, R(en, C(hng, T(rans, D(ate, Q(uit [A █
DEMO:
SYSTEM.FILER        32  8-Jan-79
SYSTEM.COMPILER     69  8-Jan-79
SYSTEM.PASCAL       38  8-Jan-79
SYSTEM.EDITOR       45  8-Jan-79
SYSTEM.PDP-11       21  8-Jan-79
SYSTEM.CHARSET       5 29-Jan-78
SYSTEM.LINKER       21  8-Jan-79
SYSTEM.SYNTAX       14  8-Jan-79
SYSTEM.LIBRARY      17  1-Jan-79
STRING1.TEXT         4  8-Jan-79
GRAPH1.TEXT          4  8-Jan-79
GRAPH1.CODE          2  8-Jan-79
TURTLE.CODE         10  1-Jan-79
QUIZ1.CODE          45  8-Jan-79
ORIENTER.CODE       12  3-Nov-78
EDITDEMO.TEXT        4 14-Dec-78
COMPDEMO.TEXT        6 26-Dec-78
STRING1.CODE         2  6-Apr-79
18/18 files(listed/in-dir), 361 blocks used, 133 unused, 124 in largest
```

Display 5.1: *An example of the display produced by the L(ist directory command of the Filer.*

an example. The numbers shown on the left of this list are the logical numbers of the I/O units. You can refer to any unit by substituting for the volume identifier with an entry like this:

    #4:

which refers to the disk in unit 4. Normally, the volume names of your floppy disk(s) will be found in units 4 and 5 in this display. The UCSD Pascal System provides space for additional floppy-disk drives starting at unit 9. I strongly suggest that you avoid using the unit number designation for referring to disks with the Filer. Doing that gives you no protection if you happen to have a different disk than you thought actually in the drive.

5.4.3 E(xtended Directory List

The E(xtended directory command is similar to the L(ist command but provides more information in its display, as shown in display 5.4. This display includes details showing where on the disk each file begins (block number) and the nature of the information stored in each file. These items are primarily of use to advanced programmers.

One other item shown by the E(xtended directory will often be of assistance to readers of this book. Note that display 5.4 shows entries marked as <unused>, along with their sizes and starting block locations on the disk. These are areas on the disk where there are no files currently allocated. They are areas that potentially could be used for additional files not yet stored on

```
Filer: G(et, S(ave, W(hat, N(ew, L(dir, R(en, C(hng, T(rans, D(ate, Q(uit [A
DEMO:
STRING1. TEXT        4   8-Jan-79
GRAPH1. TEXT         4   8-Jan-79
EDITDEMO. TEXT       4  14-Dec-78
COMPDEMO. TEXT       6  26-Dec-78
4/18 files(listed/in-dir), 28 blocks used, 135 unused, 135 in largest
```

Display 5.2: *By using a wild card specification of ":=.TEXT", the L(ist directory command shows only entries for ".TEXT" files. This screen image is based on the same directory as found in display 5.1.*

the disk. You will find that successive editing and compiling operations will eventually leave your disk with many small unused areas separating the useful files stored on the disk. When a substantial fraction of the disk is occupied by useful files, it may happen that none of the individual unused areas is large enough to provide space for a new file that needs space. If the total area contained in the several unused areas is large enough to accomodate the new file, it may be time to use the K(runch command to compress all the useful files together, leaving all the unused space at the end of the directory. The E(xtended directory command can be used to judge when it may be useful to use the K(runch command.

5.4.4 D(ate

The D(ate command is used to display the date information currently stored on the disk with which you bootload. It can also be used to change the date. Display 5.5 shows an example in which we are preparing to change the date. Our answer to the prompt will be completed when we press the RETURN key.

If you find that the date displayed by the D(ate command is correct, terminate the command simply by pressing the RETURN key, without typing in a new date. If you do supply a new date, the D(ate command will verify its understanding of the date you have typed in.

```
Filer: G(et, S(ave, W(hat, N(ew, L(dir, R(em, C(hng, T(rans, D(ate, Q(uit [A ▮
Vols on-line:
   1   CONSOLE:
   2   SYSTERM:
   3   GRAPHIC:
   4 # KB115:
   5 # DEMO:
   6   PRINTER:
   7   REMIN:
   8   REMOUT:
Root vol is - KB115:
Prefix is  - DEMO:
```

Display 5.3: *An example of the display produced by the V(olumes command of the Filer.*

Note that the format of the date you supply to the command must be "day month year" where "day" is a one- or two-digit number, "year" is a two-digit number and "month" is a three-letter abbreviation. The date command is uncompromising about this format because the program needed to accept other commonly used date formats unambiguously would occupy scarce space unnecessarily in the microcomputer's memory.

If you need to change only the day, leaving the month and year information unchanged, simply type in the one or two digits for the new day followed by RETURN. Otherwise it is necessary to enter all three items, separated by dashes.

5.4.5 P(refix

The P(refix command is used to display and/or change the default volume name prefix automatically applied by the UCSD Pascal System to file names given to it without any explicit mention of a volume name. The prompt message displayed by the P(refix command is:

   Prefix titles by what vol?

If you wish simply to display the name of the current default volume, press the

```
Filer: G(et, S(ave, W(hat, N(ew, L(dir, R(en, C(hng, T(rans, D(ate, Q(uit [A ]
DEMO:
SYSTEM.FILER       32  8-Jan-79   10  512  Codefile
SYSTEM.COMPILER    69  8-Jan-79   42  512  Codefile
SYSTEM.PASCAL      38  8-Jan-79  111  512  Datafile
SYSTEM.EDITOR      45  8-Jan-79  149  512  Codefile
SYSTEM.PDP-11      21  8-Jan-79  194  512  Datafile
SYSTEM.CHARSET      5 29-Jan-78  215  512  Infofile
SYSTEM.LINKER      21  8-Jan-79  220  512  Codefile
SYSTEM.SYNTAX      14  8-Jan-79  241  512  Textfile
SYSTEM.LIBRARY     17  1-Jan-79  255  512  Datafile
STRING1.TEXT        4  8-Jan-79  272  512  Textfile
GRAPH1.TEXT         4  8-Jan-79  276  512  Textfile
GRAPH1.CODE         2  8-Jan-79  280  512  Codefile
TURTLE.CODE        10  1-Jan-79  282  512  Codefile
QUIZ1.CODE         45  8-Jan-79  292  512  Codefile
ORIENTER.CODE      12  3-Nov-78  337  512  Codefile
EDITDEMO.TEXT       4 14-Dec-78  349  512  Textfile
COMPDEMO.TEXT       6 26-Dec-78  353  512  Textfile
< UNUSED >          9            359
STRING1.CODE        2  6-Apr-79  368  512  Codefile
< UNUSED >        124            370
18/18 files(listed/in-dir), 361 blocks used, 133 unused, 124 in largest
```

Display 5.4: *The E(xtended directory display gives additional information about each file. The extra columns show the starting disk address, block size, and type of file. Here we see the E(xtended directory display corresponding to display 5.1.*

colon (:) key followed by RETURN. For example, if you bootloaded from a volume called KB99, and have not used the P(refix command to change the default, then the P(refix command will display:

Prefix is KB99:

If you wish to change the default volume name to make it refer to a different disk, say NEWVOL, then you should answer the prompt by typing in:

NEWVOL:

followed by RETURN. As a result, a future program reference to a disk file called ANYFILE.TEXT, by lacking any explicit reference to a volume name, would have the effect of referencing the full file title NEWVOL:ANYFILE.TEXT.

5.5 T(ransferring Files from One Place to Another

The T(ransfer command is used to copy one or more files from a source device to a destination device. Most often, both devices are likely to be disks. When you press the T key, the Filer prompts with:

Transfer what file?

```
Date set: (1..31)-(Jan..Dec)-(00..99)
Today is 7-May-79
New date ? 24-MAY
```

Display 5.5: *The D(ate command just before a new date is complete. We have entered the new date of "24-MAY" in response to the query "New Date?"*

or an alternate shorter version is simply: Transfer?
if you respond with:

SRCNAME.TEXT

followed by RETURN, the Filer will again prompt with:

To where?

to which you might answer:

NEWVOL:SRCNAME.TEXT

The Filer will then copy the file SRCNAME.TEXT from your default volume over to the disk whose volume name is NEWVOL. It will continue the completion of each file transfer with a message similar to this:

OLDVOL:SRCNAME.TEXT --> NEWVOL:SRCNAME.TEXT

The T(ransfer command is used in a wide variety of commonly occurring situations, some of which are described in the following subsections.

5.5.1 Shorthand Entry of the Destination File Name

Following the initial prompt "Transfer what file?", you can type in both the source file name and the destination file name separated by a comma, as in:

SRCNAME.TEXT,NEWVOL:SRCNAME.TEXT

The effect of this is the same as the example given above, in which we waited for the second prompt message "To where?".

We can carry this a step further by using the file name duplicator character (S) as in:

SRCNAME.TEXT,NEWVOL:$

in which the dollar sign character will be interpreted as equal to "SRCNAME.TEXT".

CAUTION: If the T(ransfer command responds to your typing in the source and destination names with a message like the following:

Possibly destroy directory of NEWVOL:?

or

Destroy NEWVOL:?

or

Transfer 280 blocks? (Y/N)

then you probably have forgotten to type in even the dollar sign as an instruction of what file name to use. You should respond by pressing N for N(o, or the RETURN key. See the next subsection regarding T(ransfer in which only the volume names are used.

5.5.2 Disk-to-Disk Bulk T(ransfer

You can T(ransfer the entire contents of one disk to another by using disk volume names alone for the source and destination. For example, answer the T(ransfer command's prompt with:

SRCVOL:,DESTVOL:

to which the Filer should respond with the prompt message:

Possibly destroy directory of DESTVOL:?

in some versions just Destroy DESTVOL:?

If you wish the T(ransfer to proceed, answer with Y(es. The result will be that the disk whose volume name is currently DESTVOL will become an exact copy of the contents of the disk SRCVOL, *including even the volume iden-tification.* Any answer other than Y(es will terminate the T(ransfer command without any copy action taking place.

Since the result of a full volume-to-volume T(ransfer leaves two volumes with the same name on the UCSD Pascal System at the same time, it is impor-tant to resolve the volume name ambiguity immediately after the T(ransfer is completed. If you intend to keep both disks on line at the same time, it would be best to change the volume name of the destination disk. See Section 5.6.2 regarding the C(hange command.

5.5.3 Transferring Only Selected Files

There are two commonly used ways to transfer only a selected group of files from the source disk to the destination. You can transfer all the files whose titles begin with the characters 'SYS' from a disk called SOURCE to a disk call-ed DEST by responding to the T(ransfer command's prompt as follows:

SOURCE:SYS=,DEST:SYS=

followed by RETURN. Along the same lines, you could transfer all of the text files from your default disk to the disk called DEST as follows:

=.TEXT,DEST:=.TEXT

Note that the equals character (=) specifies all of the files on a disk if it is not qualified with additional characters as in these examples.

If you want a simplified way to review all or part of the directory of your source disk, indicating separately whether each file is to be transferred, substitute the question mark (?) for the equals character (=) in these examples. This will cause the Filer to pause after displaying each file name. If you re-spond with Y(es, the transfer of the indicated file will be carried out. Other-wise, the Filer will pass over the indicated file and go on to the next.

5.5.4 Disk-to-Disk Transfers with only One Disk Drive

Even if you have only one disk drive on your machine, the Filer will allow disk-to-disk transfer operations. The T(ransfer command first copies informa-tion from the source disk into the computer's memory. It then prompts you to remove the source disk, and to replace it with the destination disk. Next it prompts you to press SPACE as a signal to proceed by copying the contents of memory to the destination disk. In a case where the amount of information to be copied cannot fit all at once in the computer's memory, it may be necessary to substitute destination disk for source disk, and back again, several times. This will be necessary if you want to make a bulk copy of one disk to another on a one-drive machine.

5.5.5 Rearranging the Files on One Disk

The Filer provides limited facilities to allow you to reorganize the order in which files are stored on a single disk by using the T(ransfer command. Of course you can respond to the T(ransfer command's prompt with:

TESTFILE.TEXT,COPYFILE.TEXT

which will leave the old file TESTFILE.TEXT intact, but create a new file COPYFILE.TEXT on the same disk containing the same information.

If you want to move the old file, use the same title for both source and destination, as in:

TESTFILE.TEXT,TESTFILE.TEXT

or the equivalent:

TESTFILE.TEXT,$

This will cause a new copy of the oldfile to be made, and given the same directory name as the old file, and the directory entry pointing to the old copy of the file will be removed.

One common situation occurs when you have an unused area near the beginning of the directory shown at the top of the screen by E(xtended directory list, and a frequently used file near the end of the directory. Use the L(ist command to find out how many blocks this file occupies, as shown by the number displayed by L(ist in the column just to the right of the file titles. For example, let us assume that the file TESTFILE.TEXT is 23 blocks long, and that the unused area is at least 23 blocks long. You can then cause that file to be moved to the beginning of the unused area by responding to the T(ransfer command's prompt with:

TESTFILE.TEXT,TESTFILE.TEXT[23]

By placing the length of the file, in blocks, at the end of the destination title within square brackets, you tell the Filer to place the destination file as near the beginning of the destination disk as possible without overwriting any other file.

The use of T(ransfer in this manner, together with the M(ake command which is described in Section 5.6.3, can sometimes be used to force the Filer to place a copy of a file at some exact starting block number. You are not likely to need to do this unless your disk becomes damaged in some area, which then needs to be avoided. Normally, you can use the K(runch command to rearrange your disk when there are too many small unused areas, and dummy files of type ".BAD" will prevent the use of damaged areas. See Section 5.7 for additional information on handling damaged disks.

5.6 Directory Maintenance Commands

Grouped within this section are several commands used primarily to make changes in the directory which describes the files on a disk, rather than in the files. You can remove a file by deleting its directory entry and marking it unused. You can change the directory title of a file. You can make a new file by creating its directory entry and giving a title. You can compress all of the files on a disk together in the lowest numbered group of blocks using the K(runch command, thus shifting all of the unused space into one area occupying the high-numbered blocks. Finally, you can mark a disk to show its directory empty and all blocks unused with the Z(ero command.

5.6.1 R(emove

R(emove is used to eliminate one or more entries from a disk directory, leaving the space formerly occupied by the file marked unused. R(emove only change the directory, and all information stored within the file is left untouched by the R(emove command. The prompt message displayed by this command is:

Remove what file ?

or, in some versions, just: Remove?

You can respond with a single file title, or you can designate that several files are to be removed selectively. To remove the file WORK.TEXT, answer the prompt by typing in:

"WORK.TEXT"

followed by RETURN. Note that it is not sufficient to give only the simplified name of a workfile. Thus, if you have files WORK.TEXT and WORK.CODE on your disk, the R(emove command will respond with an error message if you answer the prompt by typing in only "WORK". The R(emove command does not recognize the simplified workfile name because it often happens that you may wish to remove either the .TEXT or .CODE portion of a workfile without losing the other portion.

You can R(emove several files with one use of the command by listing their titles separated by commas. For example, to remove the files ALPHA.TEXT, BETA.CODE, GAMMA.TEXT, and DELTA.TEXT, answer the prompt with:

ALPHA.TEXT,BETA.CODE,GAMMA.TEXT,DELTA.TEXT

followed at the end by RETURN. The Filer will respond with acknowledgement of its action with each file actually removed. If you misspell a file title, and the resulting title does not also exist in your directory, then the Filer will display an error message noting that the indicated file is not in your directory. A more effective way to remove groups of files in one operation is to use either of the wild card naming options. For example, to remove both the text and code portions of the workfile WORK mentioned earlier, respond to the R(emove command's prompt with:

WORK. =

Since it is common for a user to forget that other files on the disk may have the same prefix, the Filer will display the titles of all files to be removed, and then it will prompt with:

Update directory ?

You should review the list of titles actually displayed before responding with Y(es, since it may be virtually impossible to reverse a mistake in this process.

If you wish to remove various files from your directory, but cannot find a common prefix or suffix, use the question mark (?) wild card reference. The Filer will display one file title at a time, and will wait for you to answer with Y(es or N(o. For example, respond to the R(emove command's prompt with:

:?

to indicate that you want a list of all files on your default disk. To remove only files whose titles end in ".TEXT" from a disk volume called AUDIT, respond to R(emove's prompt with:

AUDIT:?.TEXT

As with the use of the equals sign wild card, the Filer will prompt at the end of the sequence to ask whether you really want to update the directory by making the indicated changes. If at some point you wish to terminate the R(emove command without making any directory changes, press the ESC key to get back to the Filer's main command world.

5.6.2 C(hange

The C(hange command is used to alter the directory titles of selected files. It can also be used to alter the name of a disk volume. The command prompts with:

Change what file ?

or in some versions just: Change?

The System waits until you type in the name of the file to be changed, followed by RETURN, and then prompts for the name to which the name is to be changed. If you answer the first prompt with:

ABC.TEXT

followed by RETURN, and answer the second prompt with:

XYZ.TEXT

followed by RETURN, the Filer should respond with:

VOL3:ABC.TEXT changed to XYZ.TEXT

or:

VOL3:ABC.TEXT --> XYZ.TEXT

assuming that the file is on a volume called 'VOL3'. You could call for the same change without waiting for the second prompt by answering the first prompt with the following:

ABC.TEXT,XYZ.TEXT

ie: by listing both the original title and the desired new title separated by a comma ,.

To change the name of a disk *volume,* use only the volume identifiers followed by colons, making no reference to any file in the directory of that volume. For example, if you want to change a volume name KB99 to NEWID, answer the C(hange command's prompt with:

KB99:,NEWID:

followed by RETURN.

The wild card file naming options can be used with the C(hange command. The portion of all orginal file titles respresented by the equal sign will be duplicated in place of the equal sign in the desired new titles. Additional title string characters may be used before or after the equal sign, or both, in either the original or desired new titles. For example, you might have a set of files WORK.TEXT and WORK.CODE and wish to change them to read OLD-WORK.TEXT and OLDWORK.CODE in order to reuse the workfile name "WORK." To do this, answer the C(hange command's prompt with:

WORK=,OLDWORK=

5.6.3 M(ake

The M(ake command is used to create a new directory entry. The command prompts with:

Make what file ?

or the shorter message:Make?

It then expects a file name as a response. Normally, you should append the number of blocks the file is to occupy on the disk, within square brackets [and], as an extension to the file title. The occasion to use M(ake sometimes arises when you wish to prevent the assignment of files to an unused area of the disk which you intend to occupy with another file at a later time. Thus you might create a new temporary file called DUMMY which you want to fill a 20-block unused area near the beginning of the disk directory. To do this, you answer the M(ake command's prompt with:

DUMMY[20]

followed by RETURN. This causes the Filer to make a new directory entry for a file called DUMMY occupying 20 blocks within the first (closest to beginning) unused area in the directory that is at least 20 blocks long. An unused area that is located closer to the beginning of the directory will be ignored if it is 19 or fewer blocks long.

If you leave out the file length specification in the brackets, the M(ake command will create a file which completely fills the largest unused area in the directory when the command is entered. If you use an asterisk '*' in place of a number in the file length specification, the M(ake command will place the new file either in one-half of the largest unused area, or in all of the second largest unused area, whichever is larger.

The M(ake command is sometimes used to change the directory information on the number of 512-byte blocks occupied by a file. The need to do this can arise if you run a program which creates a new file on the disk, but fails to reduce the space occupied by that file to the minimum number of blocks needed before terminating. Let us assume that you have some independent means available to determine how many blocks the file should occupy. If the file title is DATA, and it originally occupies 97 blocks, but you want it to occupy only 43, then use the following sequence:

A Create dummy files using the M(ake command to fill all unused areas on your disk which occur closer to the beginning of the directory than the entry for the file DATA.
B R(emove DATA. The result will be that the space occupied by DATA becomes part of the first unused area on the disk.
C M(ake 'DATA[43]'.
D R(emove the dummy files created in step (a).

5.6.4 K(runch

The K(runch command moves files toward the beginning of the disk directory in such a way as to shift all unused areas into a single, large unused area at the end of the directory. The command prompts with the following message:

Crunch what vol ?

or in some versions of the UCSD Pascal System, just:Crunch?

You should answer by typing in the name of the volume you want compressed, followed by a colon and then RETURN. For example, to K(runch the volume KB99, type:

KB99:

followed by RETURN. The Filer will then respond by displaying the message:

Are you sure you want to crunch KB99: ?

or in some versions of the UCSD Pascal System:

From end of disk, block 280? (Y/N)

where the block number in the second message will vary depending upon the size of your disk. If you respond with Y(es, the command will then move the files as commanded. Recent versions of the Filer display a message confirming the name of each file actually moved on the disk by K(runch.

CAUTION: Because the K(runch command is required to change the disk directory, and because it does not attend to this until after finishing a fairly lengthy sequence of operations, it is a dangerous command to use. If K(runch is interrupted in the midst of doing its work (power failure, damaged area on the disk, disk drive opened during operation, . . .) your disk directory will no longer correctly describe the contents of your disk. It is generally very desirable to use the B(ad-blocks command before using K(runch. See section 5.7 regarding strategies to use if your disk does in fact have bad blocks.

5.6.5 Z(ero

The Z(ero command creates a new *empty* directory on the indicated disk volume. The previous directory on that volume will be destroyed as a result of this operation. Z(ero prompts with:

Zero dir of what vol ?

or in some versions of the Filer: Zero dir of?
to which you respond with a volume identifier such as:

OLDVOL:

followed by RETURN. If the disk contains no directory, as would be the case with a new disk that never has been used previously in the UCSD Pascal System, then use the explicit unit designation in place of the volume identifier. For example, if the disk to be Z(eroed is in your spare disk drive (the one you do not use for bootloading), then respond with:

#5:

followed by RETURN. If the disk to be Z(eroed already contains an old directory, the Filer will prompt with:

Destroy OLDVOL: ?

If you answer with Y(es, the Filer will ask whether you want a duplicate directory to be created on the disk with:

Duplicate dir ?

If you respond with Y(es, the UCSD Pascal System will maintain a duplicate copy of your disk directory for possible future use in recovering from an error associated with the main directory on your disk. Any of several conditions might cause such an error, as discussed in section 5.7 of this chapter. In most cases an error in the main directory will not be reflected in the duplicate copy of the directory. A utility program COPYDUPDIR is supplied with the UCSD Pascal System for copying the duplicate directory into the main directory's area of the disk, thus allowing recovery from the error. The Filer will then ask how many blocks are to be available for files to be stored on the disk being Z(eroed. If the disk already has a directory, you will be asked to confirm with a Y(es response that the same number of blocks is again to be used. If you respond with N(o, or if the disk did not previously contain a directory, the Filer will prompt with:

# of blocks ?

or in some versions of the UCSD Pascal System:

Are there 280 blks on the disk? (Y/N)

where the number displayed depends on the size of your disk.

You should respond to the first of these messages with a number indicating the maximum capacity of the disk since the Filer has no way of knowing that capacity. If the disk is compatible with the IBM 3740 diskette (8-inch diameter, soft-sectored, single density) the number should be 494. If it is a soft-sectored, 5-1/4 inch floppy disk with 90 K byte capacity, then the number should be 167. See Appendix A for the numbers to be used with other popular machines. Note that the number of blocks given here includes a provision for the blocks occupied by the bootstrap loader, the main directory, and the optional duplicate directory, on your disk. The Filer will then ask for the volume name you want to use with the disk being Z(eroed, with the message:

New vol name ?

You should answer with an identifier (first character a letter, other characters may be letters or digits) up to 7 characters long. Use only uppercase letters to avoid an annoying bug in future references to the newly Z(eroed volume. The

Filer will prompt by asking you to verify the new volume name (since incorrectly typed volume names can lead to problems later in using the disk). If you respond with Y(es, the Filer will then write a new directory on the disk, and the Z(eroing process will be completed. You can terminate the Z(ero command following any of the prompt messages by pressing the ESC key, and no new directory will be written on the disk as a result.

5.7. Checking for Disk Errors and Repairing Them

One of the annoying facts in computing work is that secondary storage media such as floppy disks can often transmit imperfect copies of stored information when they are reread. If the information transmitted is not a perfect reproduction of the information that was originally sent to the disk, it is said to contain *errors*. If a code file contains just one 8-bit byte that is in error, that code file may be effectively useless.

There are many potential causes for errors associated with disk files. Errors can be caused by a malfunctioning disk drive, by incorrect operation of the electronic connections between computer and disk drive, by a flawed area on the recording surface of the disk, by dust or grime that has found its way into the disk's protective cover, and so on.

Some errors are marginal in nature, with the result that correct information will be transmitted on some attempts and erroneous information will be transmitted on others. A standard part of most software systems, including the UCSD Pascal System, is an arrangement whereby the data read from the disk is checked for errors. If errors are detected, the UCSD Pascal System will automatically reread the data several times in an effort to complete a read operation without any indicated errors. If rereading in this manner fails to produce an error-free copy of the data, the error is said to be *unrecoverable*. It is not unusual for a block of data to contain unrecoverable errors, when read on one disk drive, but to be readable without any errors at all when read on a different disk drive of the same type.

With careful handling of the disks and disk drives, you will usually need to contend with very few disk-related data errors. However, anyone who makes much use of a computer learns to cope with occasional errors. This section deals with two commands provided with the Filer to assist in controlling disk errors when using the UCSD Pascal System.

5.7.1 B(ad Blocks Scan

The B(ad-blocks command prompts with the message:

Bad blocks scan of what vol?

In some versions just: Bad block scan of?

You should respond with the name of the disk volume which is to be checked for bad blocks. The disk volume must be in a disk drive and ready for use when the B(ad-blocks command is invoked. This command reads each block on the disk, checking for unrecoverable errors. If there are no errors at all, you should note a *regular* clicking noise in the disk drive as the read/write head is moved from track to track. If the clicking noise comes at *irregular* intervals, there may be marginal errors in reading from the disk. If a block cannot be read without errors after many tries, the Filer will display the number of the bad block on the screen, and the B(ad-blocks command will continue scanning for additional errors.

You should take note of the block numbers where errors are found. If you have access to a second disk drive, it would be best to try the B(ad-blocks scan again using that drive. If the list of bad blocks displayed with the second drive is identical to the first list, then the signs are not good for the blocks listed. If the list differs from the first drive to the second, then the errors are likely to be marginal and quite possibly recoverable.

5.7.2 The eX(amine Command

The eX(amine command is provided as a tool to be used in repairing some types of marginal floppy disk recording errors. A common type of error arises when a disk drive uses too weak or too strong a recording signal in storing information on the disk. The problem may be the fault of either a maladjusted disk drive or of a disk with a slightly damaged recording surface. Either way, it is sometimes possible to rerecord the information, usually with a different disk drive, in such a way that it can be read without errors thereafter.

Errors on reading from a disk are usually detected through use of a check sum which is stored with each sector of information when it is recorded on the disk. The check sum is generally computed as the result of a *cyclic redundancy check* (CRC). A two-byte CRC check sum stored on the disk with the useful data is compared with a CRC check sum computed from the useful data when it is read from the disk. If the two are not equal (the recorded and recomputed CRC check sums) then a read error is detected. The UCSD Pascal System usually tries to read the same block of data, which may contain several sectors containing their own individual CRC check sums, at least 10 times in an effort to complete one read operation without a detected CRC error. Only if no error free read can be completed will an unrecoverable error be detected.

The eX(amine command tries to read the blocks you select without unrecoverable errors. If it succeeds, it then rewrites the information thus read back to the same block on the disk. It then rereads that block, and cross-compares the information read first with that obtained after the rewrite operation. If the two are the same, the Filer will inform you that the indicated block "may be okay" as a result of the operation. The eX(amine command first prompts with the message:

Examine blocks on what volume ?

or in some versions just: Examine blocks on?

After you respond with the volume name, followed by a colon and RETURN, the Filer will prompt with:

Block number-range?

in some versions, just: Block-range?
You should respond with a list of block numbers separated by commas or by giving a starting block number and a stopping block number separated by a dash character (—). For example:

234—240

followed by RETURN. The Filer will then prompt by displaying the names of all files found in the directory to include blocks within this range. It will then prompt with:

Try to fix them ?

If you respond with Y(es, the Filer will attempt the read/write operation described above on each block in the indicated group (in the example blocks 234 through 240, inclusive). If, during this operation, the Filer finds any blocks which cannot be read correctly after many tries, it will display a message stating which blocks are bad. If it prompts with:

Fix them?

and you respond with Y(es, the directory will be marked showing the damaged area of the disk to be in a file with a .BAD suffix. Subsequent K(runch operations will not attempt to move any files with the .BAD suffix.

CAUTION: Even if the eX(amine operation terminates showing that all indicated areas of the disk "may be okay," it is possible that your original information has been lost. This is possible because the error checking logic is not perfect, and the information read initially and rewritten by the eX(amine command may in fact be in error. It would be best to check the contents of your disk, with the Editor, by trying to eX(ecute a .CODE file, by checking the contents of a data file with an associated program, or by other means after using the eX(amine command.

6 Pascal Compiler - Coping with Program Errors

6.1 Goals for this Chapter

The Pascal Compiler is used to translate Pascal programs from their human readable Text form (saved on the disk by the Editor) into their directly executable code form, which the Compiler saves on the disk. The Compiler is designed to translate the entire contents of a text file in one continuous operation. Unlike the Editor and the Filer, the Compiler has hardly any interactive commands. However, it is possible to change certain controls which govern the way in which the Compiler does its work. This is done using Compiler *Directives*, which are written in the form of Pascal language comments that start with the dollar sign character ($). One of the main purposes of this chapter is to present those Compiler directives available in the UCSD Pascal System which are of use to beginning users of the system.

Also included in this chapter is a discussion of strategies for coping with program errors. If your program contains statements which fail to conform with the syntax rules of the Pascal language, the Compiler will halt at each point where it finds an error. When the UCSD Pascal System is supplied primarily for use by students, the Compiler terminates upon finding the first syntax error, and the Editor is automatically reentered with the cursor pointing at the offending item. As the System is supplied to others, the Compiler will run in a different manner intended to simplify development of large programs. You then have the option of returning immediately to the Editor to correct the syntax errors, or of continuing with the compilation to see if there are any additional errors.

Once the Compiler can go through the entire program file without finding any syntax errors, execution of the program may halt abruptly with the display of an execution error message (also called a *run-time* error message, since it occurs while the program is running). The run-time message contains coded information which can be used to find the place in the text of the Pascal program where the execution error occurred. Illustrations of both syntax and execution errors are given in this chapter, along with various suggestions on how to go about resolving the errors.

Following is a list of specific learning goals for beginners.

- Use the *include-file* option to compile a program from Pascal procedures located in two or more separate text files.
- Use the *swapping* option which allows running the Compiler on machines with a minimum amount of main memory.
- Use the Compiler's *list* option directing its output to the console display screen of your computer. Use the procedure number and byte offset values shown in the listed output to find where a run-time error has occurred.
- Place several types of syntax errors in a test program intentionally, and note how they are identified by the Compiler.

6.2 Preliminaries

The UCSD Pascal Compiler is an adaptation of the "portable" Pascal-P compiler developed by Urs Ammann at the Swiss Technical University in Zurich. The UCSD version has been substantially changed in order to run on microcomputers with restricted memory capacity, and in order to handle the UCSD extensions to the Pascal language. Like the Zurich original, the UCSD Compiler makes just one pass through the source program in a text file. The one-pass design allows the Compiler to run relatively quickly, consistent with the objective to make UCSD Pascal system as interactive as possible. However, this goal requires the Compiler to occupy a relatively large amount of memory space.

To run the Compiler, you need not only the memory space for the executable code of the Compiler, operating system, and P-machine interpreter, but also space for the working memory used by the Compiler. On most machines, the full Compiler (plus operating system and interpreter) barely fits within a total memory capacity of 48 K bytes. This leaves so little space for working memory, that only tiny programs can be compiled. To cope with this problem there are two common solutions. Of course the simplest solution, conceptually, is to add more memory capacity. A total capacity of 56 K bytes is sufficient to compile quite large Pascal programs.

The other solution causes the Compiler to be operated as if it were two separate programs which are *swapped* in and out of memory, with only one part of the Compiler occupying memory at any instant. This arrangement releases more than 5 K bytes to be used for the Compiler's working memory, and it makes 48 K a reasonable memory limit even if you want to work with fairly large Pascal programs. Unfortunately the swapping arrangement also causes the Compiler to run much slower than it does when not swapped. The reason for this is that each swap requires a large part of the Compiler's executable code to be read again from disk into memory. The degree to which the Compiler will be slowed down by swapping depends upon the type of disk you are using, and on the manner in which it is interfaced to the computer. Using standard 8-inch floppy disks, the compile speed drops from about 600 lines per minute to about 300 lines per minute in computer systems using the LSI-11 or 8085 processors.

The Compiler performs its translation tasks by breaking the source program into *tokens*. Each token is a logically separate item. Examples of tokens include identifiers (the programmer supplied symbolic names for variables, procedures, etc), individual special characters like the semicolon, comma, or equal sign, and integer or real constants (numbers). In a few special cases, two characters together comprise a token (". .", ":=", "<>", "<=", and ">="). An entire quoted string such as 'this is a string' comprises one token.

If the Compiler finds a place in the source program which fails to conform with the syntax of the Pascal language, it halts and causes a brief message to be displayed explaining the nature of the error. As it proceeds through the text of the source program, the Compiler maintains a pointer showing where the next token to be scanned begins. Thus, when an error is detected, the pointer indicates the beginning of the token immediately *following the token found to be in error*. Note that space characters in a Pascal program simply separate adjacent tokens. A space character is *permitted* between any pair of adjacent tokens. Unless both tokens are identifiers, the space is not *required*. From the point of view of the syntax, any number of adjacent space characters are considered to be the equivalent of just one separator. Also the end of one line is considered to be adjacent to the beginning of the next, and thus is considered to be equivalent to one space character in the program text. However, remember that it is not permitted to break any single token into two or more parts located on separate lines.

6.3 Comments and Compiler Directives

A *comment* may be placed in a Pascal program at any point where a space character would be permitted. In the UCSD Pascal System, a comment may begin with the character-pair "(*" and end with the matching pair "*)", or it may begin with a left curly bracket ("{") and end with a right curly bracket ("}"). As with the five two-character tokens discussed earlier, no space is allowed between the asterisk and either the left parenthesis or right parenthesis. Thus, the Compiler will not recognize

(* illegal comment *)

as a comment. However, the following would be recognized as a comment:

(* this is a legal comment *)

Of course, the main reason why comments are permitted in Pascal programs is to encourage programmers to include notes which explain what each portion of a program is intended to do. Though a well written Pascal program should be relatively easy to read and understand without comments, judiciously placed comments can greatly improve the reader's chances of understanding a program quickly and thoroughly.

While a comment embedded in a Pascal program is not considered to be part of the program, and thus does not constitute tokens to be translated into executable object code, it is possible for the Compiler to extract information from the characters contained within a comment. The UCSD Pascal Compiler recognizes any comment that begins with a dollar sign character as a directive to the Compiler itself. Note that the dollar sign must be the first character following "(*" or the left curly bracket ("{"). There can be no intervening SPACE characters.

Compiler directives are instructions to the Compiler which cause it to change selected switches controlling the way it operates. For example, the Compiler is capable of sending a specially formatted copy of the source program text to a printer, or to a disk file for later printing, or even directly to the computer's console video display. This formatted output adds substantially to the time taken by the Compiler to complete its program translation tasks. Consequently the formatted output is normally not activated. However, the source program can contain a Compiler directive, the list directive, instructing the Compiler to begin generating the formatted output. If the slower formatted output is not needed throughout the entire source program, another Compiler directive can be included at the appropriate point in the source program to deactivate the formatted output thereafter. Details on the list directive will be given in a later section of this chapter.

6.4 Include Directive

Sometimes it is convenient to keep portions of a Pascal program in separately edited text files. The include directive tells the Compiler to regard the entire text contained in a named text file as if it were part of the source program text at the point where the include directive occurs. For example, in the following small piece of a program:

```
    PROGRAM TEST;
    VAR X, Y, Z;
    BEGIN
(*$I PREAMBLE.TEXT*)
    IF X> =100 THEN
        •
        •
        •
```

"$I" would instruct the Compiler to treat all of the program statements contained in a file called PREAMBLE.TEXT as if they had been included within the text of the program at the point immediately following "BEGIN."

One situation in which one might use the include directive occurs when one wants to develop several programs, all of which are to have an identical section of program statements. Of course, if the included file is changed, then all of the programs which use the include directive referring to that file will have to be recompiled in order to take advantage of the changes.

Occasionally, one wants to include a file which contains CONST, TYPE, VAR, PROCEDURE, and FUNCTION declarations. If the program file containing the include directive must also have its own set of declarations, it is implied that there must be a relaxation of the Pascal syntax requirement that CONST declarations occur before TYPE declarations, TYPE must occur before VAR, and so on. The UCSD Pascal Compiler allows relaxation of this strict sequence in the special case in which the include directive occurs between the last variable declared in a VAR list, and the first PROCEDURE or FUNCTION heading declared in the main program.

For reasons associated with the limited amount of memory available on most microcomputers, the UCSD Pascal Compiler cannot handle an include directive embedded within the text of a file which itself is included.

The include mechanism also requires the Compiler to establish a buffer memory area to be used with the included file, and also to allocate memory for other special purposes. As a result, the include directive may not be of any practical use on some machines which have no more than 48 K bytes of main memory.

Display 6.1 An example of the Compiler's output display showing a syntax error.

6.5 The Compiler's Display and the List Directive

As the Compiler works its way through the text of the source program, it is capable of generating two kinds of displayed or printed output designed to assist a user in keeping track of its progress. The principal uses of this output are associated with program debugging, and will be discussed further in later sections of this chapter.

Normally, the Compiler displays only a very terse summary of its progress as it goes through the source program. Display 6.1 provides an example.

```
 1    1    1:D     1 (*$L CONSOLE:*)
 2    1    1:D     1 PROGRAM EDITDEMO;
 3    1    1:D     3 VAR G1,
 4    1    1:D     3    G2,
 5    1    1:D     3    G3,G4:INTEGER;
 6    1    1:D     7    B1,B2,B3:BOOLEAN;
 7    1    1:D    10
 8    1    2:D     1 PROCEDURE REPEAT1;
 9    1    2:D     1 VAR S,SG:STRING;
10    1    2:D    83    L,N:INTEGER;
11    1    2:0     0 BEGIN
12    1    2:1     0    WRITELN(
13    1    2:1     0       'TYPE ANY STRING FOLLOWED BY <RET>'
14    1    2:1     3       );
15    1    2:1    53    READLN(S);
16    1    2:1    72    N:=1;
17    1    2:1    75    L:=LENGTH(S);
18    1    2:1    81    REPEAT
19    1    2:2    81       SG:=COPY(S,1,N);
20    1    2:2    97       WRITELN(SG);
21    1    2:2   116       N:=N+1;
22    1    2:1   122    UNTIL N>L
23    1    2:0   124 END (*REPEAT1*);
24    1    2:0   144 █
```

Display 6.2 When the list directive is activated the compiler will produce a formatted listing of the program. Here is an example using the console output device for display.

In this display, a line with the following appearance:

< 10> . . . .

shows how many lines of Pascal source text have been compiled so far. One period is displayed for each line compiled, as the line is being compiled. The number within brackets at the left margin is the number of lines already compiled at the time when this line begins to be displayed.

A line with the following appearance:

REPEAT1 [1844 words]

shows the name of the procedure or function body (executable statement part) which the Compiler is just beginning to translate. It also shows the number of 2-byte memory words still available for use by the Compiler for working storage. Most of the Compiler's working storage is used to keep a table of the declared identifiers that are currently usable within the program. You should notice a marked reduction in the available storage space when compiling a program which employs a large number of declared identifiers.The output generated by the list directive is illustrated in display 6.2.

In addition to showing the text of the source program as it is being compiled, on a line-by-line basis, this display also includes formatted information of potential use in program debugging. The list option is activated by the directive:

(*$L CONSOLE:*)

which may be seen in the top line of display 6.2. "CONSOLE:" is the volume identifier of the main system display on output operations (it also is used for input from the keyboard). In its place you could put any desired disk file title, making sure to use the suffix ".TEXT". The resulting file will contain the formatted listing generated by the Compiler in a form that can be read using the Editor. If your machine has a "PRINTER:" or "REMOUT:" volume, substitute either volume name for "CONSOLE:" to have the listing sent to an external printer or other remote terminal device.

The list option can be deactivated by the directive:

(*$L − *)

In display 6.2, the number displayed at the left is the number of the program text line being compiled. Next to the right is the digit "1" on each line. This is the number of the program *segment*. Separately compiled program segments provide a means of controlling *overlays* in the UCSD Pascal System, ie: a means to conserve on memory space when working with large programs. The rules on preparing programs containing separately compiled segments are beyond the scope of this book, but they are described in the main reference manual for the UCSD Pascal System.

To the right of the segment number, there is a number immediately followed by a colon. This number is assigned by the Compiler as a unique identification of each program block (procedure or function) within a segment. The main program is always block number 1. The block numbers are assigned in the order of appearance of the PROCEDURE and FUNCTION headings. The order of appearance of the procedure and function identifiers in the Compiler's normal display corresponds to the appearance of the executable parts of each block, and thus may not be the same as the order of block number assignments.

Immediately to the right of the colon is the character "D" (in lines that pertain to the declarations) or a number (in lines containing executable program statements). A number indicates the level of *nesting* of Pascal statements, and it may be useful in finding unmatched BEGIN . . . END pairs in a program.

The final column of numbers, located just to the left of the Pascal program statements proper, is to be interpreted differently depending upon whether the associated lines are declarations or executable statements. On a declaration line, the number tells how many 2-byte memory cells intervene between the base address of the block and the first declared identifier in a group. Unfortunately, the "first" declared identifier in a list such as G1, G2, G3, G4 in display 6.2 is really the identifier that we read as last, ie: G4. Thus G4 is at location 3, G3 is at location 4, G2 is at location 5, and G1 is at location 6. The next location, 7, is allocated to B3 in this example. These location numbers will be of very little use to beginning users of the UCSD Pascal System. They are intended for use with a debugger program capable of displaying a *dump* of the program's working memory contents.

On a line containing executable statements, the number in the last column tells how many bytes of compiled code were generated before the first code bytes of the current line started being generated. These numbers can be of considerable assistance to a beginner who is searching for the source of a run-time error in a program. We will explore that topic in some detail in a later section.

6.6 Miscellaneous Compiler Switch Directives

All of the miscellaneous Compiler switch directives tell the compiler to start or stop doing something as it goes through the source program. In each case, the directive is selected using a single character followed by either a plus character ("+") to turn the switch "on," or a minus character ("−") to turn the switch "off." For example:

(*$S+*)

turns on the Compiler's swapping mode, which conserves memory space. On the other hand:

(*$S−*)

turns swapping off.

6.6.1 Enable GOTO Directive

For reasons associated with the teaching approach used in the Bowles textbook cited in Chapter 1, the Compiler normally prevents the use of the Pascal GOTO statement. GOTO statements are considered a potent source of errors in program logic, and their use should be avoided wherever possible. On the other hand, there are occasional situations where the GOTO can be used to provide an escape from an error situation in such a way as to allow a program to run more efficiently. For that reason, the UCSD Pascal Compiler can be conditioned to allow the GOTO statement through use of the "G+" directive, ie:

(*$G+*)

6.6.2 I/O Check Switch

As supplied to users, the UCSD Pascal System terminates a program abnormally in the event of an error encountered during an input/output (I/O) operation. The Compiler can be instructed not to generate the code which checks on the result of an I/O operation using the option:

(*$I − *)

Means are available then for the programmer to provide program checks to determine how to cope with an I/O error. This subject is beyond the scope of a book for beginners. Details may be found in the main reference manual for the UCSD Pascal System. Unless you find it essential to do your own checking for I/O errors in a program, I strongly urge you to forget about the I/O check switch directive! However, its use *is* discussed in this book in Chapter 8, "Programming to use Disk Files."

6.6.3 Quiet Compilation Switch

If your computer's principal console device is a hard-copy printer rather than a display terminal or if your display is restricted to run at hard-copy speeds, you may want to suppress the Compiler's normal progress messages in order to save time. The UCSD Pascal System has a control switch called "SLOWTERM" which, if set to true, indicates that you have a slow terminal device. The Compiler's quiet switch directive suppresses normal progress messages if it is turned on. If your copy of the UCSD Pascal System has SLOWTERM set to true, then the quiet switch will automatically be turned on. If not, you can produce the same effect with the directive:

(*$Q + *)

Conversely, if you want to turn off the suppression of progress messages, use the directive:

(*$Q − *)

The status of your SLOWTERM control switch can be changed using the utility program SETUP, which is supplied with the UCSD Pascal System. SETUP is a self-documented program which provides its own instructions. You may have to step through various irrelevant option switches using SETUP before you reach the SLOWTERM option. The program provides a command that allows you to avoid reviewing all the remaining options after changing SLOWTERM.

6.6.4 Swapping Mode Switch

The swapping mode switch directive causes the Compiler to be executed as if it were two separate programs which alternate in their use of the same area of the computer's memory. This allows the Compiler to be used on a machine with roughly 5 K bytes less main memory than would otherwise be required to compile a program of any given size. It also has the undesired effect of making the Compiler run less than half as fast as it otherwise would run in the absence of the swapping switch. The name of the option describes the swapping back and forth of the two parts of the Compiler. If you intend to use the swapping mode option, the following line must be the first line of your text file (following any optional comments):

(*$S+*)

Unlike some of the other switch directives, the swapping mode cannot be turned on and off at will during a compilation. It must remain on for the entire compilation if the option is to be used at all.

For some microcomputers with restricted amounts of main memory, the UCSD Pascal System will be supplied to users with the swapping switch option turned on by default. If you have a copy supplied in this way, you can turn swapping off (if that makes any sense given the memory available to your computer) using the directive:

(*$S−*)

Recent versions of the Compiler begin compiling with the swapping mode turned off, but invoke swapping when it is needed to allow the compilation to continue. With this feature, you can forget about the (*$S+*) directive.

6.7 Syntax Errors

If the Compiler finds a section of program text which fails to conform with the syntax rules of Pascal, it halts and causes an error message to be displayed. If the STUDENT option switch of the operating system is set to true, the first syntax error will cause the Compiler to terminate and turn over control to the Editor automatically. Use the SETUP program, which is largely self-documented, to reset the STUDENT option to false. An example of the display you should expect to see is shown in display 6.1, which refers to a sample program called COMPDEMO, which is supplied as one of the files in the standard UCSD Pascal System disks.

In display 6.1, the right-parenthesis character ")" which should have been placed just to the left of the semicolon has been left out of the program. The Compiler's progress display contains copies of the line where the program error is found (up to the token where the Compiler notes the error) and the previous program line. The symbol "< < < <" amount to a cursor pointing to the token found to be in error.

The bottom line shown in display 6.1 notes the number of the line where the syntax error is found, gives the code number of the error, and then provides several options. If you press the E key, to invoke the E(dit option, the result will be the same return to the Editor that takes place automatically when the STUDENT option switch of the operating system is set to true. In that case, a message briefly describing the nature of the syntax error will be displayed at the top of your screen (assuming that there is a copy of the file SYSTEM.SYN-

TAX on your bootload disk). This is shown in display 6.3 which replicates the
Editor's display resulting from this operation. The Editor's cursor is left pointing at the same position where the symbol "< < < <" pointed when the Compiler halted. You can continue at this point to use the Editor by pressing the
space bar.

```
')' expected.  Type <sp>
FUNCTION BLOWUP(X,Y:INTEGER):BOOLEAN;
VAR
    I,LB,UB:INTEGER;
    CH:CHAR;
    A:ARRAY[1..10] OF INTEGER;
BEGIN
    LB:=X;
    UB:=Y;
    FOR I:=LB TO UB DO
        BEGIN
            A[I]:=I*I;
            WRITELN(I,':    ',A[I] ;█
        END;
    BLOWUP:=UB ) 10;
END (*BLOWUP*);

BEGIN (*MAIN PROGRAM*)
    WRITELN('START EDITDEMO');
    WRITELN;
    REPEAT1;
    WRITELN;
    REPEAT2;
    WRITELN;
```

*Display 6.3 Screen editor display (small file version) after a syntax is detected by the Compiler, and the user is
returned to the Editor.*

The two other command options made available by the Compiler, as shown
in display 6.1, are intended for use in working with large programs. If you
press the space bar when the Compiler has halted, the Compiler will continue
attempting to compile the rest of the program. Because of the nature of the
Compiler, this may or may not be a sensible thing to do. Some syntax error
conditions leave the Compiler confused, and all it can do is to produce an
unending sequence of error messages at the same program location. Other error conditions are not as drastic and the Compiler can sometimes continue all
the way to the end of the program with no problem. If you suspect that the
Compiler has become confused after a sequence of syntax error conditions,
you can terminate further compilation without automatically invoking the
Editor by pressing the ESC key while the Compiler is halted.

The bottom line in display 6.1 contains only the coded number of the syntax
error, and not the explicit error message displayed in the top line by the Editor
as seen in display 6.3. The main reason for this is that provisions to show an
explicit error message in the Compiler's display would require the use of additional program memory. Since the Compiler is already almost too big to fit
within a 48 K byte memory (along with the operating system and interpreter),
the decision was made to leave out the explicit error message at this point. A

complete list of the numbered syntax error messages used in UCSD Pascal System may be found in Appendix D1 of this book.

If you are working with a large Pascal program, it may be most efficient to use a printed listing of the program as an aid during compilation. When the compiler halts and shows an error message, write a brief note about the error at the place in the listing where the error occurs. Then instruct the Compiler to continue by using the space option. Continue noting your errors until the compilation has been completed, or until it is obvious that the Compiler has lost its way. This method saves the time that would otherwise be taken in multiple switching back and forth from Compiler to Editor to Compiler. . . . It also simplifies the process that you *should* go through after noting each error — ie: the visual search for errors similar to the one just flagged by the Compiler.

The following subsections provide suggestions on how to find some of the more troublesome syntax errors that often arise in the use of the UCSD Pascal System.

6.7.1 Unmatched BEGIN . . . END Pairs

One of the more common errors in writing Pascal programs is the failure to match each BEGIN in a source program with a corresponding END. The problem is exaggerated when one uses a display screen for most program editing work, since then it is often the case that both BEGIN and matching END cannot be displayed on the screen at the same time. While the Compiler has no trouble discovering that each BEGIN has not been matched with an END (or vice versa), it generally points to the problem at a point far removed from the place in the source program where the error is actually caused. Display 6.4 illustrates the problem.

```
       67   1     5:D      9   A:ARRAY[1..10] OF INTEGER;
       68   1     5:0      0   BEGIN

BLOWUP    [ 1720 words]
(  68)    69   1     5:1      0    LB:=X;
       70   1     5:1      3    UB:=Y;
       71   1     5:1      6    FOR I:=LB TO UB DO
       72   1     5:2     18       BEGIN
       73   1     5:3     18          A[I]:=I*I;
       74   1     5:3     32          WRITELN(I,':  ',A[I]);
       75   1     5:3     85          (*END;*)
       76   1     5:3     85       BLOWUP:=UB ) 10;
       77   1     5:2     90    END (*BLOWUP*);
       78   1     5:2     97
       79   1     5:1     97 BEGIN (*MAIN PROGRAM*)
       80   1     5:2     97    WRITELN('START EDITDEMO');
       81   1     5:2    131    REPEAT2;
       82   1     5:2    133    WRITELN;
       83   1     5:2    141    IF BLOWUP(5,15) THEN
       84   1     5:3    149       WRITE('Upper Bound too large');

      WRITE('Upper Bound too large');
   END. <<<<
   Line 84, error 6: <sp>(continue), <esc>(terminate), E(dit
```

Display 6.4 Syntax Error caused by BEGIN not matched by END.

Upon return to the Editor, the full error message that is displayed reads:

Illegal symbol (possibly missing ';' in line above)

Considering that the actual error occurs 13 lines earlier in the program, at line 75, this message is far from helpful.

The section of program that is shown here is the same as shown in display 6.3, but the missing right parenthesis has been correctly restored in line 74. Line 75 shows the END enclosed as a comment, thus preventing the Compiler from regarding the END as part of the program. The Compiler thus goes on translating, and regards the END in line 77 as matching the BEGIN in line 72, even though the comment in line 77 makes it clear to a human reader that this END was intended to be the closing token of the BLOWUP function. The Compiler carries on assuming that the subsequent lines are still part of the BLOWUP function. This can be seen by the fact that program code generation (the right-most column of numbers) does not start from zero upon entering the main program block in line 79. Another indicator is that the main program statements are all shown as part of block #5 in the block-number column of the display.

The failure to match END's with their corresponding BEGIN's is often a difficult error to trace to its cause when working with a large program. The block number and bytes-generated columns of the Compiler's list option provide a mechanism which should help materially to find these errors.

6.7.2 Comment Not Completed with a Closing "*)" Symbol

In a similar vein, it is all too easy to forget to finish a comment with the necessary closing ((*)" or "#" symbol. Display 6.5 provides an illustration. In this case, the actual error occurs on line 77, where an asterisk has been left out. The Compiler does not detect an error until line 80. The message corresponding to error 14 reads:

; expected (possibly on line above)

Again not very helpful. Since correct syntax clearly does not require a semicolon on line 79, we must look for other evidence.

Again we notice that the Compiler failed to start generating code at the opening BEGIN of the main program block (line 79), instead showing that 96 bytes of code had been generated in block 5 at that point. The block number should be 1, since line 79 is the first line of executable code in the main program block, and the byte-count should be 0. See line 68 for the corresponding correct byte count for block 5.

In this case, the error is relatively easy to detect by noting the failure of code generation to start over at the beginning of a new block. Another common indicator is the failure to advance the bytes-generated counter from line to line in an area of the program which contains a sequence of executable statements. When this occurs, something has clearly happened to prevent the code generation. Usually the reason is an incomplete comment.

```
      62   1    3:0   184
      63   1    5:D     3 FUNCTION BLOWUP(X,Y:INTEGER):BOOLEAN;
      64   1    5:D     5 VAR
      65   1    5:D     5   I,LB,UB:INTEGER;
      66   1    5:D     8   CH:CHAR;
      67   1    5:D     9   A:ARRAY[1..10] OF INTEGER;
      68   1    5:0     0 BEGIN

BLOWUP    [ 1720 words]
( 68).    69   1    5:1     0   LB:=X;
          70   1    5:1     3   UB:=Y;
          71   1    5:1     6   FOR I:=LB TO UB DO
          72   1    5:2    18     BEGIN
          73   1    5:3    18       A[I]:=I*I;
          74   1    5:3    32       WRITELN(I,':   ',A[I]);
          75   1    5:2    85     END;
          76   1    5:1    92   BLOWUP:=UB > 10;
          77   1    5:0    97 END (*BLOWUP );
          78   1    5:0    97
          79   1    5:0    97 BEGIN (*MAIN PROGRAM*)

BEGIN (*MAIN PROGRAM*)
   WRITELN <<<<
Line 79, error 14: (sp)(continue), (esc)(terminate), E(dit
```

Display 6.5 Errors can be caused by improperly using or omitting the closing delimiter in a comment, as shown here.

6.7.3 Nested IF Statements

Nested IF statements are an invitation to make syntax errors, some of which the Compiler is unable to detect. Display 6.6 provides an example of a *correct* small program for use in seeing how some of the errors arise.

In this case, one of the best clues for checking correct program construction is the column of numbers representing depth of nesting, ie: the numbers immediately to the right of the column of colon characters. Notice that the nesting depth is increased by 1 each time a statement controlled by another is entered. It is reduced by 1 when the same controlled statement terminates. For example, the IF statement in line 9 controls the IF statement starting in line 10. Line 9 is at level 1, while line 10 (the controlled statement) is at level 2. The ELSE in line 12 refers back to the IF . . . THEN in line 10, and hence is shown at level 2. The compound statement (BEGIN . . . END) starts in line 13 at level 3, being controlled by the IF . . . THEN . . . ELSE . . . at level 2, and it ends in line 16, again at level 3.

Now consider display 6.7, in which we have placed an additional BEGIN . . . END pair to make the program logic a little more obvious. This program is still correct, and carries out the same steps shown in display 6.6. However, the additional compound statement brings an additional level of nesting. Thus the new BEGIN in line 10 of display 6.7 is at level 2, while the IF . . . THEN in line 11 is at level 3. This same IF . . . THEN had been at level 2 in display 6.6.

The addition of extra BEGIN . . . END pairs is often useful when working with a complicated set of nested IF statements as a way to force the program logic to go as one plans. If the extra compound statement is redundant, as in display 6.7, no harm is done since the Compiler generates no corresponding code. However, the extra compound statement makes it unnecessary for the programmer to trace back through the nested IFs to make sure that the ELSE in line 17 of display 6.6 (line 19 of display 6.7) belongs to the IF . . . THEN in line 9 of both figures.

```
     2    1    1:D     1 PROGRAM IFBOMB;
     3    1    1:D     3 VAR W,X,Y,Z:INTEGER;
     4    1    1:0     8 BEGIN

 IFBOMB  [ 1905 words]
 (   4)   5    1    1:1     8   WRITE('Enter value of W:'); READLN(W);
     6    1    1:1    49   WRITE('X:'); READLN(X);
     7    1    1:1    81   WRITE('Y:'); READLN(Y);
     8    1    1:1   113   Z:=0;
     9    1    1:1   116   IF W > X THEN
    10    1    1:2   121     IF W > Y THEN
    11    1    1:3   126       Z := W
    12    1    1:2   126     ELSE
    13    1    1:3   131       BEGIN
    14    1    1:4   131         IF W = Y THEN
    15    1    1:5   136           Z := Y
    16    1    1:3   136       END
    17    1    1:1   139   ELSE
    18    1    1:2   141     Z := X;
    19    1    1:1   144   WRITELN('Z=',Z);
    20    1    1:0   176 END.

 20 lines, 8 secs, 157 lines/min
 Smallest available space = 1905 words
```

Display 6.6 A program containing nested IF statements with no errors.

Unfortunately, one sometimes decides to clarify a set of nested IF statements by using extra compound statements after getting a large part of the nested structure into the program via the Editor. Thus, a common error is to add the END but forget the corresponding BEGIN that should be placed earlier in the program. Display 6.8 provides an illustration.

The extra END appears on line 17. It should be matched by a BEGIN between lines 9 and 10. The END on line 17 is indented two columns less than line 16, a natural step to take when increasing the indentation by two for each additional statement level, and decreasing the indentation correspondingly for each statement level terminated. This time the Compiler again generates the ubiquitous "illegal symbol" message (error 6), which is virtually equivalent to "something is wrong but I don't see what."

The clue to look for in this situation is the level numbers on lines 15, 16, and 17. Since the level is shown as 0 in line 17, the Compiler considers this END to be the match for the BEGIN in line 4, ie: the opening BEGIN of the block. But visual inspection of the program, if a reasonable effort at logical indentation has been made in writing the program, quickly shows that it had not been intended that the END in line 17 would be the closing END of the block. Otherwise that END would have been placed in the program with no indentation. At this point we trace back, and discover that the level 3 statements are properly balanced, but that there is no BEGIN at level 2 to match the END in line 17. Since the nested IF structure began at level 1 in line 9, the END should necessarily have matched a BEGIN at level 2 somewhere after line 9. Thus the problem is narrowed quickly to the point where the infraction effectively took place.

```
Command: E(dit, R(un, F(ile, C(omp, L(ink, X(ecute, A(ssem, D(ebug,? [II.0]

IFBOMB   [ 1905 words]
(   4).      5  1    1:1      0   WRITE('Enter value of W:'); READLN(W);
         6  1    1:1      49  WRITE('X:'); READLN(X);
         7  1    1:1      81  WRITE('Y:'); READLN(Y);
         8  1    1:1      113 Z:=0;
         9  1    1:1      116 IF W > X THEN
        10  1    1:2      121    BEGIN
        11  1    1:3      121       IF W > Y THEN
        12  1    1:4      126          Z := W
        13  1    1:3      126       ELSE
        14  1    1:4      131          BEGIN
        15  1    1:5      131             IF W = Y THEN
        16  1    1:6      136                Z := Y
        17  1    1:4      136          END
        18  1    1:2      139    END
        19  1    1:1      139 ELSE
        20  1    1:2      141    Z := X;
        21  1    1:1      144 WRITELN('Z=',Z);
        22  1    1:0      176 END.

22 lines, 8 secs, 164 lines/min
Smallest available space = 1905 words
```

Display 6.7 *The nested IF program of display 6.6 showing an extra BEGIN ... END pair.*

```
PASCAL Compiler [II.0.A.1]
(   0).      1  1    1:D      1 (*$L CONSOLE:*)
         2  1    1:D      1 PROGRAM IFBOMB;
         3  1    1:D      3 VAR W,X,Y,Z:INTEGER;
         4  1    1:0      0 BEGIN

IFBOMB   [ 1905 words]
(   4).      5  1    1:1      0   WRITE('Enter value of W:'); READLN(W);
         6  1    1:1      49  WRITE('X:'); READLN(X);
         7  1    1:1      81  WRITE('Y:'); READLN(Y);
         8  1    1:1      113 Z:=0;
         9  1    1:1      116 IF W > X THEN
        10  1    1:2      121    IF W > Y THEN
        11  1    1:3      126       Z := W
        12  1    1:2      126    ELSE
        13  1    1:3      131       BEGIN
        14  1    1:4      131          IF W = Y THEN
        15  1    1:5      136             Z := Y
        16  1    1:3      136       END
        17  1    1:0      139 END

    END
    ELSE <<<<
Line 17, error 6: (sp)(continue), (esc)(terminate), E(dit
```

Display 6.8 *An example of a set of nested IF statements with an unmatched extra END statement, leading to a compile error.*

```
Command: E(dit, R(un, F(ile, C(omp, L(ink, X(ecute, A(ssem, D(ebug,? [II.0]
(   0).    1    1    1:D    1 (*$L CONSOLE:*)
        2    1    1:D    1 PROGRAM IFBOMB;
        3    1    1:D    3 VAR W,X,Y,Z:INTEGER;
        4    1    1:0    0 BEGIN

IFBOMB  [ 1905 words]
(   4).    5    1    1:1    0   WRITE('Enter value of W:'); READLN(W);
        6    1    1:1   49   WRITE('X:'); READLN(X);
        7    1    1:1   81   WRITE('Y:'); READLN(Y);
        8    1    1:1  113   Z:=0;
        9    1    1:1  116   IF W > X THEN
       10    1    1:2  121     IF W > Y THEN
       11    1    1:3  126       Z := W
       12    1    1:2  126     ELSE
       13    1    1:3  131       IF W = Y THEN
       14    1    1:4  136         Z := Y
       15    1    1:3  136     ELSE
       16    1    1:4  141       Z := X;
       17    1    1:1  144   WRITELN('Z=',Z);
       18    1    1:0  176 END.

18 lines, 7 secs, 147 lines/min
Smallest available space = 1905 words
```

Display 6.9 An example of nested IFs with BEGIN . . . END missing.

Next, let's see what happens if one neglects to put in both the BEGIN and the END in a situation where the program logic is changed as a result. This is illustrated in display 6.9.

In this illustration, the ELSE in line 15 has been left indented as if it belongs still with the IF . . . THEN in line 9. However, if that were true, then the level of line 15 would be 1, as associated with the same ELSE in displays 6.6 and 6.7. Since the level in line 15 is actually 3, it is clear that the ELSE associates back to the IF . . . THEN in line 13, thus having quite a different effect than it did in the preceding displays. Here, there has been no error of syntax detectable by the Compiler, but there may well have been an error of program logic detectable because the level entries are not consistent with the indentation used when editing the program.

6.8 Execution (Run-Time) Errors

An execution error occurs at *run-time*, ie: while a program is running, if the program attempts an illegal action. A list of the execution errors detectable by the UCSD Pascal System is given in Appendix D2 of this book. The most likely error in most programs is a "value range error," indicating that the program tried to assign a value outside the declared range of an array index or subrange variable. Other common errors are "stack overflow" (to run out of working memory space), "integer overflow" (attempting to assign an integer value larger than can be expressed within a 16-bit memory word), "divide by zero," and "string too long."

When a run-time error occurs, the System halts and displays a three-line error message on the principal console device. The top line displayed is one of the messages tabulated in Appendix D2. The second line contains an entry such as:

S# 1, P# 4, I# 14

meaning that the program halted in segment 1, procedure (block) 4, and at a code offset of 14 bytes from the beginning of the block. These numbers correspond to the numbers in the second, third, and fifth columns of the Compiler's list option output.

As a concrete example, consider displays 6.10 and 6.11. Display 6.10 shows a section of the program file COMPDEMO. Not shown is the statement which calls the function BLOWUP, in which the variable X is given the value 5, and Y the value 15. Display 6.11 shows the output of this program. The top few lines in display 6.11 result from the parts of COMPDEMO which have simply been copied from the EDITDEMO program used in Chapter 4.

```
59   1   3:3   148     READLN(S);
60   1   3:2   167   END;
61   1   3:0   169 END (*REPEAT2*);
62   1   3:0   184
63   1   5:D     3 FUNCTION BLOWUP(X,Y:INTEGER):BOOLEAN;
64   1   5:D     5 VAR
65   1   5:D     5   I,LB,UB:INTEGER;
66   1   5:D     8   CH:CHAR;
67   1   5:D     9   A:ARRAY[1..10] OF INTEGER;
68   1   5:0     0 BEGIN
69   1   5:1     0   LB:=X;
70   1   5:1     3   UB:=Y;
71   1   5:1     6   FOR I:=LB TO UB DO
72   1   5:2    18     BEGIN
73   1   5:3    18       A[I]:=I*I;
74   1   5:3    32       WRITELN(I,':   ',A[I]);
75   1   5:2    85     END;
76   1   5:1    92   BLOWUP:=UB > 10;
77   1   5:0    97 END (*BLOWUP*);
78   1   5:0   112
79   1   1:0     0 BEGIN (*MAIN PROGRAM*)
80   1   1:1     0   WRITELN('START EDITDEMO');
81   1   1:1    36   WRITELN;
```

Display 6.10 A compiler list option display of the function BLOWUP.

At the bottom of display 6.11, we see that the program "blew up" (also called *bombing* or *abending*) in segment 1, block 5, and at a point in the code 24 bytes from the beginning of the block. Referring to display 6.10, we see that this offset occurs within line 73, which starts in byte 18 and ends in byte 31. Since the error was a "value range error," we immediately suspect the index value I in the subscripted array variable A[I]. There are no other items in line 73 which would correspond to a value range error. Now we trace back through the program to see where I might have taken on a value outside the range 1..10 which was declared in line 67. Since the value of UB is initialized to the value of Y when the function was entered, and since the value of Y is 15, we see that the FOR statement will inevitably generate a value of 11. This is the first value outside the declared range, and hence is the value which will trigger the value range error. We cross-check this conclusion with the displayed output of the program itself in display 6.11. The program ran long enough to display lines for values of I ranging from 5 through 10, but it failed to continue to display values from 11 through 15. Thus the conclusion is confirmed that the value range error arose because of a value of I outside the allowed range.

As an exercise, try using a similar method to find the error in the REVERSE procedure of the same program. This can be found by running the program, and by responding to the second prompt message with a string which contains an *even number* of characters, for example "even."

Of course, not all execution errors are as easy to find as the errors illustrated in this section. The error message allows you to find out which block contains the statement where the program finally blew up. It may then be necessary to insert extra WRITELN statements into the program to determine the values of essential variables at times immediately *before* the execution error occurs. These values may or may not make sense relative to the program logic, and it may be necessary to go back to earlier points in the program, again with extra WRITELN statements, to determine how the essential variables took on the offending values.

```
Running...
START EDITDEMO

TYPE ANY STRING FOLLOWED BY <RET>
ANY
A
AN
ANY

TYPE ANY STRING FOLLOWED BY <RET>

5:   25
6:   36
7:   49
8:   64
9:   81
10:  100

Value range error
S# 1, P# 5, I# 24
Type <space> to continue
```

Display 6.11 *Running COMPDEMO in order to show a run-time error gives this display.*

7 Quizzes for Pascal Self Study

7.1 Goals for this Chapter

A set of automated interactive quiz programs is available for use coordinated with study of the textbook *Microcomputer Problem Solving Using Pascal*, by K L Bowles, Springer-Verlag publishers, New York and Heidelberg, 1977. The quizzes are to be available in a separate package from distributors of the UCSD Pascal System. All of the quizzes will be available in both self-study and class-study (grades recorded) versions.

Our main goal in this short chapter is to introduce the two styles of quizzes that are available. One style contains drill-and-practice exercises designed to review the principal study goals of Chapters 1 through 5, and 7 through 11, of the Bowles textbook. The other style provides automated testing for correct execution of small programs written as procedures or functions. The drill-and-practice quizzes are generally self-documenting. The programming quizzes are accompanied by brief specification sheets, each of which states the problem to be solved by one of the testable programs.

If you are a beginner seeking to make effective use of the UCSD Pascal System, your goal should be to go through all of the quizzes, repeating if necessary until you pass each one. If you are using this book in connection with an organized class, your instructor will specify how to use the automated quizzes.

7.2 Drill-and-Practice Quizzes

Each of the drill-and-practice quizzes are supplied as a ".CODE" file, and associated ".DATA" file, for use with a special testing program. The quiz programs are designed to run under Version II.1 of the UCSD Pascal System, and later versions which include facilities for "Intrinsic Units." (Though Version III.0 has a higher number, it does not have Intrinsic Units.) To use the testing program, you need the files:

```
TESTER.CODE
TESTER.DATA
SYSTEM. LIBRARY
```

The SYSTEM.LIBRARY file must contain the Intrinsic Units designed for use with the quiz programs.

The directory names of the quiz programs have an obvious connection with the associated chapter in the Bowles textbook. For example, QUIZ8.CODE and QUIZ8.DATA are for use with chapter 8. To use this quiz, go to the "Command:" world, press X (for eX(ecute), and then respond to the prompt with:

```
TESTER
```

followed by RETURN, in the usual manner. The TESTER program prompts you with a request for the number of the textbook chapter for which you want quizzes.

Please note that the information shown in this book has been displayed on a display screen having 80 column lines. The quizzes will also be available in slightly altered versions for 40-column displays like that on the Apple II computer.

When you answer the TESTER's prompt, instructions for the first of several quiz questions will appear after a short delay for reading the quiz materials from the disk. Each drill-and-practice quiz contains several questions, which are selected in random order when you run the program.

Each question is itself a subprogram (Pascal procedure or function) which selects the detailed information presented on the screen from a random pool of quiz data. Therefore, each time a particular question is presented, the detailed information in the question will vary, and/or the order in which the information is presented will vary. In effect, each question subprogram can generate hundreds or thousands of similar questions which differ in their detailed subject content.

Display 7.1 shows the display generated by one of the questions in QUIZ1, at a point when we have partly completed the required answers to the question.

```
Question 2  Identifiers


    Indicate, by typing Y(es) or N(o) (and then
    (RET) ), whether each of the following examples is
    an (identifier) obeying the PASCAL syntax rules
    In this question, each example is either
    EXACTLY ONE (identifier) OR something else

    To pass this question you must answer 10
    examples correctly before getting 10 wrong

            (number correct: 1    wrong: 0)

    QUIZ#8    ? N

        THAT'S CORRECT

        Special character '#' not allowed



            Press RETURN to continue,(ESC) to Quit
```

Display 7.1 A display generated by an identifier question of Quiz #1.

The philosophy of each of the quiz questions is to encourage you to practice answering factual questions until you indicate a reasonable mastery of the subject matter. Thus, you are generally permitted at least one chance to answer a question, or part of a question, incorrectly without failing the question. If you do answer incorrectly, the quiz program will repeat with the same subquestion or a similar subquestion at a later time. The self-test quiz program will allow you to try each question twice. It will give a summary when the program terminates, showing how many questions you answered correctly and how many you failed. A passing grade for the entire quiz will be indicated if you fail no more than two questions as presented. Since each question is repeated once if you fail it the first time, this means that you generally will have to pass each question correctly once in order to pass the quiz as a whole.

In the question presented in display 7.1, you answer each choice with Y(es or N(o. The program responds by indicating whether your answer is correct. You are required to answer ten choices correctly with no intervening wrong answers. As an incentive to analyze the displayed strings, to indicate whether they are legally constructed identifiers, the question will be failed if you get 10 answers wrong before you get 10 correct in a row.

Display 7.2 illustrates a second question from Quiz #1. This question uses a modified multiple-choice strategy. The program displayed by the question contains some lines that are correct and some that are incorrect because they violate the Pascal syntax rules. The selection of right or wrong for each line is random, and thus will vary each time the program is run. The question asks you to consider a specific line of the program displayed. It then displays a statement about that line. If the statement correctly describes that line, then answer Y(es. Otherwise answer N(o, and the question will display another choice.

```
Question 1:  Syntax.
     1:  PROGRAM APIS61;
     2:  START
     3:  WRITELN('This', 'is a demonstration');
     4:  WRITELN('of ''PASCAL'' program execution');
     5:  WRITELN('Type <CR> to cont.'); (* await response *)
     6:  CLEARSCREEN
     7:  MOVE(-5)
     8:  PENCOLOR(BLACK),
     9:  MOVE(5);
    10:  TURN(90, -100);
    11:  TURN(DOWN),
    12:  MOVE(30);
    13:  READLN;
    14:  WRITELN('Bye for now');
    15:  ( GOODBYE )
    16:  END
            TALLY:  Correct - 1     Wrong - 0

Is line 2:
INCORRECT because of Quote(s) missing (y/n)? █
```

Display 7.2 A program syntax question from Quiz #1.

For each line you are asked to consider, there are *several (multiple)* choices. The order in which the choices are presented is random, and thus varies each time the question program is run. In this case, you are required to answer for 5 lines *correctly*, in order to pass the question. If you answer incorrectly, the "wrong" count will be increased by 1, and the "correct" count will be reset to zero. Unlike the multiple choice questions that are familiar to most students, this "concealed multiple choice" approach makes it almost impossible to pass a question by guessing the answers, one must analyze them.

Display 7.3 illustrates a question that requires the operator to type in a string of characters folowed by RETURN. Display 7.3 is a snapshot of the screen just after we have entered an incorrect string, as seen on the third line on the right side of the display. The question program compared our input string, typed into that line, with a string generated internally by the question program itself. Since the two were not equal, the question program then displayed the expected (ie: correct) answer as shown.

Display 7.4 shows a repeat of the same question program which occurred later in running the same quiz. This time we have typed a correct answer where prompted to do so on the third line on the right side. The question program displays a message of congratulation at the bottom of the screen, and it then waits for a RETURN before terminating.

Display 7.5 illustrates another question from Quiz #2, in this case one that requires simple integer constants as answers.

```
Question 2:  Procedures
    PROGRAM QUIZ2;
    VAR X:CHAR;
      PROCEDURE P(CH:CHAR);
      BEGIN
        WRITE('P:',CH,',');            Enter the EXACT sequence of characters
      END (*P*);                        that should be displayed by the program
      PROCEDURE Q(CH:CHAR);            QUIZ2:P:N,R:N,Q:Z,
      BEGIN
        WRITE('Q:',CH,',');
        P(CH);                         Sorry, the expected answer is
      END (*Q*);
      PROCEDURE R(CH:CHAR);            P:N,R:N,Q:Z,P:Z,
      BEGIN
        P(CH);
        WRITE('R:',CH,',');
        Q('Z');
      END (*R*);
    BEGIN
      X:='N';
      R(X);
    END
                  Press RETURN or space to continue, (esc) to quit.█
```

Display 7.3 Question from Quiz #2 requiring a string to be typed in.

```
Question 1:  Procedures
    PROGRAM QUIZ2;
    VAR X:CHAR;
      PROCEDURE P(CH:CHAR);
      BEGIN
        WRITE('P:',CH,',');            Enter the EXACT sequence of characters
      END (*P*);                        that should be displayed by the program
      PROCEDURE Q(CH:CHAR);            QUIZ2:Q:G,P:G,
      BEGIN
        WRITE('Q:',CH,',');
        P(CH);
      END (*Q*);
      PROCEDURE R(CH:CHAR);
      BEGIN
        P(CH);
        WRITE('R:',CH,',');
        Q('T');
      END (*R*);
    BEGIN
      X:='G';
      Q(X);
    END
                  Fantastic!  Press RETURN or space to continue, (esc) to quit █
```

Display 7.4 Question shown in display 7.3, but with correct answer.

```
Question 1  Arith Express.
          Answer 3 correctly without intervening errors.
          Three wrong answers terminates the question.

     Given

          VAR W, X, Y, Z  INTEGER;

     and

          W =4;
          X =3;
          Y =2;
          Z =2;

                    Right: 3  Wrong: 0

     Enter the value of the following arithmetic expression ? 11

                    (W+X)+Y*Z

                    Press RETURN to continue, (escape) to quit.
```

Display 7.5 Quiz #2 question requiring numeric answers.

Finally, after completing (either correctly or incorrectly) all of the questions presented by a Quiz program, the program will display a summary showing how you fared. Display 7.6 illustrates this summary in a case where we failed the Quiz by getting too many questions wrong.

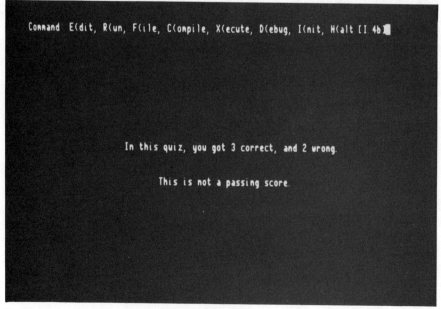

```
Command  E(dit, R(un, F(ile, C(ompile, X(ecute, D(ebug, I(nit, H(alt [I 4b]
```

```
               In this quiz, you got 3 correct, and 2 wrong.

                    This is not a passing score.
```

Display 7.6 Summary displayed at end of a quiz session.

7.3 Programming Quizzes

Each of the programming quizzes is accompanied by a specification describing a problem for which you are to write a Pascal program as the solution. In each case, the specification includes an exact description of input and output parameters (or the type of a function) designed for use with a program which tests whether your program actually solves the problem correctly. In the self-test versions of the quiz system, the tester program should be executed in the usual way. For the programming quizzes, the TESTER program expects to find an executable SYSTEM.WRK.CODE file containing the executable procedure or function that you want to have tested.

As an example, one programming quiz asks for conversion of a decimal number, expressed as a string of decimal characters, into an octal number, expressed as a string of octal characters in an output parameter (variable). Display 7.7 illustrates part of the solution to the problem, shown as an Editor display with part of the program lines missing.

```
)Edit  A(djst C(py D(lete F(ind I(nsrt J(mp R(place Q(uit X(chng Z(ap  [E.6]
PROGRAM DUMMY;
▌
SEGMENT PROCEDURE STUPROC(VAR SOURCE:STRING);
VAR OCTAL:STRING;
  BADCHAR:BOOLEAN;

PROCEDURE DECTOOCTAL(INN:STRING; VAR OUT:STRING);
VAR I,X,DIGIT:INTEGER;
  CH:CHAR;
  S:STRING[1];
BEGIN
  OUT:='*';  (*Error here*)
  FOR I:=1 TO LENGTH(INN) DO
    BEGIN END;
END (*DECTOOCTAL*);

BEGIN (*MAIN PROGRAM*)
  OCTAL:='';
  DECTOOCTAL(SOURCE,OCTAL);
END (*STUPROC*);

BEGIN
END
```

Display 7.7 Part of solution program for Programming Quiz 12A.

Notice that the procedure containing the solution is headed with:

SEGMENT PROCEDURE STUPROC(. . .

where "SEGMENT" is a reserved identifier which tells the Compiler to translate this procedure so that it can be called into execution by another program. The entire heading line for this procedure must be exactly as specified in the information sheet accompanying the programming quiz.

In most respects, you develop (Edit and Compile) the solution program for a programming quiz in the same manner that you develop other programs in the UCSD Pascal System. To fool the Compiler into thinking that you are compiling a complete program, you must supply a dummy PROGRAM heading, and a dummy compound statement to take the place of the executable part of the main program block. Thus the format of the complete solution program is:

```
PROGRAM DUMMY; (*any name is ok*)
(* any required TYPE declarations go here *)
SEGMENT PROCEDURE STUPROC( (* specified parameters here *) );
VAR
   . . .
BEGIN
   . . .
   executable body of STUPROC
END (*STUPROC*);
BEGIN (* dummy main program body *)
END.
```

Display 7.8 shows the display generated by the TESTER program after testing an incorrect solution to the decimal-octal conversion problem. In this case, we deliberately caused the error by inserting an irrelevant asterisk character in the output string. You may notice that the amount of information the TESTER program can give you is very limited concerning what went wrong in your program. Display 7.9 illustrates the display for a sorting problem, in which slightly more information is available from TESTER.

```
Command: E(dit, R(un, F(ile, C(omp, L(ink, X(ecute, A(ssen, D(ebug,? [I.5
Enter the unit number please - 12
Which quiz version in that unit are you testing? A
Testing in progress.


Well... What can I say?  Your procedure didn't work right.
 I passed you decimal '1734' and the procedure returned '1734'
The correct answer is '3386'
```

Display 7.8 Display generated by TESTER for decimal-octal problem.

```
Command E(dit, R(un, F(ile, C(omp, L(ink, X(ecute, A(ssem, D(ebug,? [[ 5]


LIST           YOUR ANSWER    CORRECT ANSWER

'YES'          'YES'          'JELLY'
'MOUND'        'MOUND'        'KIND'
'PEEL'         'PEEL'         'LIFT'
'LIFT'         'LIFT'         'MONKEY'
'ORDER'        'ORDER'        'MOUND'
'WOULD'        'WOULD'        'ORDER'
'JELLY'        'JELLY'        'PEEL'
'KIND'         'KIND'         'VERY'
'VERY'         'VERY'         'WOULD'
'MONKEY'       'MONKEY'       'YES'


As you can see, your procedure did not work.
```

Display 7.9 TESTER display for incorrect sort problem solution.

The TESTER program can help you to find out what went wrong with your solution, but it cannot point out the reason for the error within your program. In general, TESTER is programmed to call your procedure several times with various input data values chosen to test for special cases. Most beginning programmers find it all too easy to write a program which solves a specified problem for *typical* data values, but which fails to cope with certain values that can sometimes occur. TESTER tries to test for correct handling of all of the special cases that can occur within the range of the specified problem.

In debugging your solution for a programming quiz problem, you may find it helpful to write your own *driver* program to call your SEGMENT procedure or function. There is no hidden magic associated with the required dummy program heading or its executable body. Thus, you can add program statements which turn the DUMMY program into a complete executable program which calls your SEGMENT procedure or function, passing your own input data for testing. You can run or execute this program in the normal manner. When you think that you have the program running correctly, you can then try executing the TESTER program to evaluate your solution.

NOTE: All variables and procedures used by your SEGMENT procedure or function must be declared within that procedure or function. If declared globally as part of the main DUMMY program heading, they will not be available to your procedure or function when it is called by the TESTER program. The results if you do this will be unpredictable!

Another debugging strategy is the use of WRITELN statements embedded within your solution program to trace the values of important variables as the program is executed. In this way, you can follow the steps your program takes in working with the data, and often can find the point where the program fails to do what is needed correctly. You can also insert extra READLN statements, which cause processing to halt until you press the RETURN key, to freeze the display at strategic points so that it can be studied. Note that the TESTER program will scan through your source program looking for READLN statements, and several other statements related specifically to the problem version. TESTER will not pass you if it finds one of these "forbidden" statements. The objective is to reject problem solutions which use tricks to avoid developing the program logic required by the problem specification. You can complete your debugging of a program using the extra READLN statements, then remove those statements after the program appears to run correctly. TESTER should then award a "pass" for the correct solution.

8 Programming to Use Disk Files

8.1 Goals for this Chapter

Perhaps the single most important area of applications programming of concern to users of the UCSD Pascal System is the handling of disk files. Whether your interest is in business data bases, word processing, experimental data collection, process control, or some other field, you are likely to need to work with disk files. None of the published textbooks currently available, including the Bowles textbook cited in Chapter 1, contains information designed to help beginners make use of disk files in their Pascal programs.

The main goal of this chapter is to provide an introduction to programming for disk files using the UCSD Pascal System. It is unfortunate that the present accepted standard definition of the Pascal language lacks facilities for several important aspects of disk file handling. Since UCSD Pascal extends the standard language to allow random access handling of disk files, *readers are warned* that some of the facilities described in this chapter will not be found in all Pascal systems, or will differ in those systems.

Specific learning goals for this chapter include the following steps:

a) Create a new disk file containing structured records.
b) Update selected records in the file created in step (a).
c) Using a Pascal program, create a new text file on disk. Read the contents of this file using the Editor.

d) Process the data contained in the file contained in step (c), changing selected data within that file. Read the contents of the altered file to check your results.

e) Write a program capable of running without abnormal termination, even if certain disk processing input/output errors are encountered.

Note: This chapter does not provide a comprehensive review of all kinds of disk-oriented input/output facilities that are available with the UCSD Pascal System. Readers interested in going further should obtain the main reference manual for the UCSD Pascal System.

8.2 Overview

Disk files are coming to be used almost universally in small general-purpose computer systems. The disk storage devices now available range from the smallest of the mini-floppy disk drives, capable of storing roughly 90 K bytes, up to the very large multidrive hard disk systems, capable of storing billions of bytes. The UCSD Pascal System has been designed from the beginning with floppy disks in mind. The System is also being used on hard disk based machines, but generally in a mode which logically simulates one or more floppy disk drives.

While both disks and tapes are used as secondary magnetic storage media for computers, and share some characteristics, the disks have an important advantage in allowing relatively fast random access to a record located anywhere within a file. In contrast, access to an arbitrarily chosen record on a tape file may require minutes of tape movement before that record can be reached. The program development facilities of the UCSD Pascal System are designed to take advantage of the random access characteristics of floppy disks. While the System can be used, in principle, with tape files, they cannot be used as the main secondary storage device which supports interactive program development.

Disk files are commonly used for any and all of the following purposes:

- Storage of information one wishes not to lose when the computer is turned off.
- Storage of files of information too large to fit within the computer's main memory all at once.
- Saving data representing the status of a partially completed long computing task. This permits restarting the task without repeating the entire computation, should the task be interrupted for any reason.
- Communication of files of data from one machine to another via physical transportation of the disks themselves.

In programming to use disk files one must be concerned about several levels of detailed information. On one level, the physical characteristics of the disk medium and the mechanical drive on which it runs are important. The relationship of these characteristics to the UCSD Pascal System, and the resulting file decriptions are the subject of Section 8.3

In Pascal, a file is an ordered sequence or collection of data items all of which are of the same declared type. In this sense, a file is similar to an array. Unlike an array, a Pascal file may contain a variable number of data items. Moreover, the time required for a program to gain access to any one data item in a file may range from tens of milliseconds (ie: hundredths of a second) to several tenths of a second. The time taken to access an item in an array is typically only a few tens of microseconds (ie: tens of millionths of a second). Because of these differences, the means of handling the storage of data into Pascal files, and retrieval of data from those files, is very different from the handling of Pascal arrays.

The data items stored in Pascal files are often composed of structured data types, usually Pascal Records. Formally, a file may be composed of items declared to be of any type that can be declared in the language. One exception is that a file of items that are themselves files is generally not allowed. A special file type of considerable importance among Pascal users is the Text file, which consists of a stream of single character items broken into lines. Generally a text file is accessed sequentially whether on disk or on tape rather than by random record selection.

Pascal language facilities for handling files take the form of built-in procedures and functions. The philosophy surrounding these procedures and functions in the accepted standard definition of Pascal (See Jensen & Wirth, cited in Chapter 1) is oriented to the use of magnetic tape files. UCSD Pascal includes two additional built-in procedures (SEEK and CLOSE), and slightly altered definitions of those in the standard language in order to provide random disk access following a philosophy very close to that of the standard language. These changes are considered controversial among language specialists in the Pascal community, and should be regarded as unique to UCSD Pascal. Other Pascal implementations use their own approaches, each typically altering the standard language in subtle but different ways. For this reason, *readers are strongly urged to isolate their uses of input/output references* to disk files in a small number of easily modified procedures and/or functions. This will reduce the effort needed to modify a program developed in UCSD Pascal for use in another system.

Section 8.4 of this chapter presents the built-in facilities of Pascal for working with disk files composed of structured data. Wherever practical, without detracting from the readability of the presentation, differences between standard Pascal and UCSD Pascal are pointed out.

Section 8.5 applies the built-in facilities to random access handling of disk files.

Section 8.6 discusses text files with particular attention to their storage on disks. Since text files are byte-stream oriented, they may also provide the best means of handling input/output connected with a wide variety of peripheral devices, including those interfaced to the UCSD Pascal System by users themselves.

Section 8.7 discusses error recovery, a troublesome but extremely important topic. Disks and tapes provide imperfect media for the storage of data, and it is generally necessary to provide means for coping with errors. Errors can be made in the process of recording data on a disk, in reading the data back from the disk, or even in passive storage intervening between recording and reading.

Section 8.8 provides a preliminary overview of a number of library facilities that should eventually become available with the UCSD Pascal System for working with disk files. These include Sort, Merge, and Indexed Sequential Access routines. The capability to provide these facilities selectively, thus using up scarce memory space only when they are needed, is a recent addition to the System. Now that this capability is available, it is anticipated that the library of specialized routines for use with UCSD Pascal will grow rapidly.

8.3 Physical Description of UCSD Pascal Disk Files

Data is recorded on magnetic disks for digital computers in a manner reminiscent of recording on home phonograph records. In both cases, the information is contained in a large number of (nearly) circular tracks. The tracks of a phonograph record actually form one long spiral track. On a computer disk, the tracks are separate concentric circles which are not connected with each other.

Digital information is stored on a computer disk within a thin magnetic recording surface very similar to the surface of a magnetic recording tape. The important difference between a computer disk (or tape) and a cassette tape intended for playing back music is the manner in which the information is expressed electronically. On a computer disk, the manner of recording is designed to store binary digital information with a very low probability that errors will be made on playback.

Within one of the tracks on a computer disk, the data is stored as a stream of binary bits. Usually, the stream of bits is a multiple of 8-bits long, and logically considered to be a stream of 8-bit bytes. Typically, the full capacity of one track on a floppy disk is about 4000 bytes. On a hard disk, it can be substantially larger. Usually, the disk is made to rotate continuously, because the time delay to start the disk drive spinning fast enough for data to be read can be at least several seconds. The rate of rotation results in the transfer of data between disk and computer so fast that it cannot be processed while the transfer is under way. Transfer rates for floppy disks range generally from roughly 20,000 bytes per second to more than 60,000 bytes per second. Transfer rates for hard disks run from about 300,000 to more than one million bytes per second.

This high transfer rate generally requires that there be some means for transferring only part of a track between disk and computer during any single read or write operation. On the first industry-wide standard floppy disks (the 8-inch diameter disks compatible with IBM's model 3740), each track is broken up into 26 *sectors*, where each sector stores 128 bytes of data. To keep the cost of the interface equipment connecting the computer with the disk drive as low as possible, each sector in this design contains additional information for controlling errors and for identifying the *address* number of the sector. In the IBM design, the disk has a total of 77 tracks. Data transfers are initiated by the computer's operating system software, based on requests from user programs, and require specifying both the track number, and the number of the sector wanted within the track.

Later floppy disks brought to the competitive marketplace have varied the original IBM design in many ways. There are mini-floppies (5¼ inch diameter), double- and single-sided floppies, double-density floppies (compared with the original IBM density, ie: number of bytes per track), *hard-sectored* floppies (which substitute guiding holes punched in the disk for the *soft-sector* addressing information described above), and sector sizes differing from the original 128 bytes. Moreover, the order in which the sectors are numbered within a track for addressing purposes varies from machine to machine for reasons having to do with efficiency.

8.3.1 Sector Interleaving

On many microprocessor-based machines, the disk interface hardware is relatively simple and leaves much of the logic to be carried out by the computer's central processor. This makes it impossible to read or write two or more adjacent sectors on the disk during a single rotation. If sectors in adjacent *locations* going around one track are given numbers in sequential 1, 2, 3, 4, ... order, the result can be to force a full rotation of the disk in between read or write transfers involving sectors with adjacent *numbers.* Transfers of groups of sectors with adjacent numbers are so common that the numbering is often arranged to provide a physical separation between sectors with adjacent numbers. Thus, the (logical) sector number sequence on one track might be 1, 14, 2, 15, 3, 16, ... In reading the sequential sectors 1, 2, 3, ... there is a time delay between finishing the read of one sector, and starting the next, because of the rotation time associated with the intervening sector not found in that sequence. For example, after finishing the read of sector 2, there is a time delay for sector 15 to be passed over before reading of sector 3 can begin. This time delay is used by the computer's central processor to catch up with its work associated with the read operation. In that way, it becomes possible to read a second sector after wasting only 1/26th of one disk revolution (for the IBM 3740 compatible diskettes), rather than having to wait for more than one complete revolution if the sectors were in adjacent physical locations.

Not all floppy disk-based machines use alternate sector *interleaving* such as that just described. Some have hardware fast enough that interleaving is not required. Others use three-way, four-way, or other interleaving factors.

8.3.2 512-Byte Blocks — Universal Units of Disk Transfer

Since the UCSD Pascal System is designed to run on a wide variety of machines, the scheme used for transferring data between disk and computer is logically *transparent* to virtually all of the floppy disk variations just describ-

ed. Instead, the System regards all disk files as if they were composed of
blocks 512-bytes long. In this respect, a block can be thought of as if it were a
logical sector. The System interacts with the hardware through a set of low
level driver routines known as the "Basic I/O Subsystem," or BIOS. The BIOS
accepts a request for transfer of a numbered block, and takes care of collecting
the actual sectors on the disk which in combination make up the block. From
the point of view of the operating system (the control software part of the
UCSD Pascal System), all disk input/output transfers take place via 512-byte
blocks. Details of how the BIOS for each different machine copes with the
actual physical sectors on the disk are of no direct concern to the software,
nor to most programmers.

The blocks on a disk are given successive integer numbers starting at 0 and
counting upwards, ie: 0, 1, 2, 3, 4, ... Since the number of sectors on one
track often does not work out to provide capacity exactly equal to an integer
multiple of 512-bytes, some blocks overlap two tracks. The BIOS is expected
to accept a block number, and to handle all the details of making the
equivalent of that block out of the sectors actually stored on the disk. The
operating system retains an area of memory called a *buffer* for each file which
is in use. The buffer has capacity to store one complete block. The upper part
of Figure 8.1 illustrates this part of the process.

8.3.3 Structured Logical Records

Of course it is recognized that very few programmers will find it convenient
to declare a Record type for their disk files that just happens to be exactly 512
bytes long. It is much more usual for the length of a Record to be less than 512
bytes and not evenly divisible into 512 bytes. Also, some Records are longer
than 512 bytes, but not an integer multiple of 512.

To provide maximum flexibility for the Pascal programmer, the UCSD
Pascal System takes care of packing logical typed Records into the 512-byte
blocks when writing to the disk, and unpacking the Records when reading
from the disk. All of the necessary bookkeeping is done so that the programmer does not need to be directly concerned with the calculation of which
block(s) any logical Record will occupy. Moreover, a logical Record may
overlap from one block of another, allowing full use to be made of the storage
capacity of each block in the file except for the last one which usually is only
partially occupied.

As a result, the user's Pascal program needs only to request access to a
specific logical record in a file by using its number. For reading the N-th logical
record from the file, Figure 8.1 shows how the operating system and BIOS
routines team up to transfer just the requested Record into the *window
variable* associated with the file. A similar process takes place in the reverse
direction when writing to the disk. For a discussion of programming fine
points associated with the file and its window variable, see Section 8.4 of this
chapter.

Sometimes the logic of a program will make it desirable to include Records
which are declared to be laid out quite differently, mixed together within the

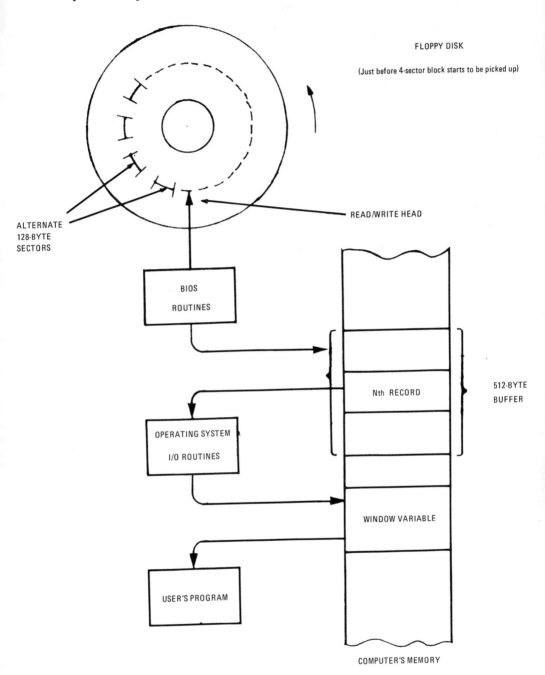

FLOPPY DISK

(Just before 4-sector block starts to be picked up)

READ/WRITE HEAD

ALTERNATE
128-BYTE
SECTORS

BIOS

ROUTINES

512-BYTE

BUFFER

Nth RECORD

OPERATING SYSTEM

I/O ROUTINES

WINDOW VARIABLE

USER'S PROGRAM

COMPUTER'S MEMORY

Figure 8.1 Illustration of steps invoked on read of N-th record.

same file. Pascal allows you to declare that the last field of a Record type has
several different *variants*. For example, we might want to mix together records
on people and on inventory items within the same file. We might also want to
slip an occasional note into the file in the form of a long packed array of
characters not broken into independent fields. The declarations associated
with these records might appear as shown in listing 8.1.

```
TYPE RECTYPE=(PERSON,INVENTORY,MEMO);
   PERSREC=
      RECORD
         NAME,COMPANY:STRING[32];
         STREET:STRING[20];
         CITYSTATE:STRING[30];
         TEL:PACKED ARRAY[0. .9] OF CHAR;
         BALANCE:INTEGER[8]
      END;
   INVREC=
      RECORD
         ITEMNAME:STRING[40];
         PLANT:INTEGER;
         LOCATION:PACKED ARRAY[0. .3] OF CHAR;
         VALUE:INTEGER[6];
         DATE_ACQUIRED:PACKED ARRAY[0. .5] OF CHAR
      END;
   NOTEREC=PACKED ARRAY[0. .131] OF CHAR;
   RECDEF=
      RECORD CASE RECTYPE OF
         PERSON:(PERS:PERSREC);
         INVENTORY:(INV:INVREC);
         MEMO:(NOTE:NOTEREC)
      END;
VAR
   RD:RECDEF;
```

I will defer until Section 8.4 any Pascal programming consideration of how
to associate these Record types with a file. Notice that the type PERSREC
occupies a total of 136 bytes (strings include a length field; the total length of a
string variable must fill an even number of bytes), INVREC occupies 58 bytes,
and NOTEREC 132 bytes. Since the UCSD Pascal System has no way to
enforce which of the three types will occupy the *variable* RD at any instant, it
is necessary for RD to occupy the maximum record size regardless of which
type occupies RD. A similar consideration makes it necessary for a file constructed on disk from variant type records to use the size of the largest variant
as the size of all records stored on the disk. In our example, this would mean
that a substantial amount of disk space would be wasted if a large part of the
file actually consisted of records of the INVREC type.

If you consider using disk storage for large numbers of records using several different Record types which differ markedly in size, it probably would be best to create separate files in order to save space. This is a situation where tape files have an advantage in that variable length records only occupy enough space on the tape to accomodate their individual sizes. Variable length records could also be arranged to occupy only their individual sizes on a disk.

This would imply either that access to these records would have to be sequential (ie: not random), or that a relatively complex indexing scheme would have to be used. The only simple method available in the UCSD Pascal System for storing variable length records on disk files uses text files, as discussed in the following subsection.

8.3.4 Text Files

The conceptual view of a text file in Pascal is that it consists of an indefinite number of lines, each line being composed of an indefinite number of characters followed by an end-of-line marker. In this section we present a brief discussion of how this concept is implemented in the UCSD Pascal System. Programming details are deferred until Section 6 of this chapter. Most beginners who follow the Pascal rules on text files will have very little reason to be concerned with the file characteristics described in the rest of this section. They are presented here for those curious enough to get into trouble if they do not understand these details. The details will also be helpful to readers who wish to write programs which transfer text data between the UCSD Pascal System and another system which uses simpler text file conventions.

In many small computer systems which use the fixed length block scheme for disk storage, the storage of text information within the blocks is very simple. The characters in each line are written into a block-sized buffer area in memory until the block fills up. The block is then transferred to the disk, and the buffer cleared for additional characters. The remaining characters on the line are then written into the buffer, and the end-of-line marker is also written into the buffer. Unfortunately, there is no standard end-of-line marker used in the computer industry. One common scheme uses the two character sequence CR LF, where "CR" is the ASCII carriage return character, and "LF" is the ASCII line feed character. (ASCII is the American Standard Code for Information Interchange.) Others use just a single CR or LF character, and still others use characters selected from the ASCII set or from other codes.

The design of text files in UCSD Pascal has been strongly influenced by the requirements of the screen-oriented Editor. The objective was to make the Editor as fast and user-responsive as possible. Several of the design decisions have made UCSD Pascal text files less similar to text files in other popular microcomputer systems than is probably necessary. Some of the loss in Editor responsiveness associated with the simple popular text file formats could be made up using carefully chosen built-in (assembly language) procedures made available to the Editor (which is a large Pascal program). Thus, the description given here applies to UCSD Pascal text files in their form at the time this book is being written (mid-1979). In future versions of the UCSD Pascal System, it is possible that some changes will be made.

The principal differences between UCSD Pascal text files and the simpler format found on most small systems are as follows:

- The end-of-line character is a single ASCII CR character.
- Blank characters at the beginning (left side) of a line are compressed into an *indentation code* which consists of an ASCII DLE character (decimal value is 16) followed by a character representing the number of blanks. The decimal equivalent value of this second character is 32 plus the number of blanks represented by the code. The indentation code-pair is missing if there are no blanks at the beginning of a line.
- The text is written into the disk file in two-block logical records called *pages*, 1024 bytes long.
- No line of text is split between the end of one page and the beginning of the next. Instead, the empty space at the end of a page, which is too short to accomodate the line that would otherwise start there, is filled with ASCII NUL characters. The binary or decimal value of a NUL character is zero.
- Page number zero of a text file is reserved for control information used by the screen Editor. Text is stored in a text file starting at the beginning of page number one. Unless you use special I/O facilities intended for advanced users of the UCSD Pascal System, a Pascal program using a text file will not be able to refer to the contents of page zero.

Note that the page-oriented layout and the page zero requirement are the reasons why the minimum size of a text file in the UCSD Pascal System is 4 blocks.

8.4 Working with Structured Data Files

The general philosophy associated with input/output operations in Pascal is conceptually similar to the model of a magnetic tape file. In this concept, the usually imaginary tape is seen as resting in a position such that one record of the type associated with the file will be transferred upon the next request for an input or output operation. The record is transferred from the tape to a special *buffer variable* associated with the file as a result of executing a GET statement. Similarly, the content of the buffer variable is transferred to the tape as a result of executing a PUT statement. The pointer indicating where the tape is positioned is advanced by the length of one record when GET or PUT is executed.

In UCSD Pascal, as in standard Pascal, repeated execution of GET results in successive transfers of records in the sequence in which they are recorded on a disk. In standard Pascal, PUT may only be executed when the position pointer is at the current end-of-file position. One reason for this rule is that computer tape drives are not generally built to allow overwriting a previously written record within a file. Since UCSD Pascal is designed for work with disk files which do allow overwriting records within a file, repeated execution of PUT is allowed as long as the file's position pointer indicates a record location within the range allocated to the file. UCSD Pascal provides a built-in SEEK statement for assigning a new value to the file's position pointer. Standard Pascal provides no equivalent of the SEEK facility.

All Pascal input and output data transfers take place via the buffer variable. Hence the buffer variable is sometimes referred to as a *window* through which the file may be viewed. The window, ie: buffer, is treated as if it were an ordinary variable for purposes of assigning value to or from that variable within the Pascal program. However, the buffer variable behaves unlike ordinary variables in the sense that certain input/output operations leave the content of the buffer variable undefined, even when a value has previously been assigned by the Pascal program.

Pascal READ and WRITE statements are really composite statements constructed using GET and PUT respectively, in addition to implicit assignment statements involving the file's buffer variable.

In addition to dealing with the actual transfer of data to or from a disk file, the programmer also has to be concerned with instructions to the operating system on how the file should be handled. Until a file is *opened* (readied by the system for either input or output) using a Pascal RESET or REWRITE statement, the UCSD Pascal operating system does not allocate space for the 512-byte buffer illustrated in Figure 8.1. Moreover, it is necessary for the program to inform the operating system what directory name is to be associated with a file. The file declaration specifies the program's internal identifier and record type. However, the same file in the same program can be made to refer to many different disk files, each having a different directory name. In UCSD Pascal, the RESET and REWRITE statements of standard Pascal have been extended to provide the means for the program to communicate the file's directory name to the operating system. This allows one program to compute the directory names of several different files, each being associated with the same internal file identifier in the program at separate times. For each declared file variable, only one of the actual disk files can be *open* at one time for input and/or output transfers.

Since there are several possible dispositions of a disk file after it has been used in a UCSD Pascal program, the program must generally inform the operating system how to *close* the file. This is done using the CLOSE statement, a UCSD extension to the language which does not exist in standard Pascal. CLOSE with the LOCK option requests the operating system to retain the directory entry of a new file for future use. If LOCK is not used, a file newly created by the program will be regarded as temporary, and the disk space it occupies during the program execution will be marked as unused when the CLOSE action takes place. In addition to controlling the disposition of a file's directory entry, the CLOSE statement also informs the operating system that it may release the buffer space associated with the file for other uses. A CLOSE without LOCK is automatically invoked if no CLOSE statement has been explicitly executed before termination of the block (procedure or function) in which the file is declared.

Because the number of data items stored in a file may vary, it is necessary to provide a facility whereby a Pascal program repetition statement involving input or output may be told when to stop. For structured data files, the only facility provided for this purpose in standard Pascal is the built-in function EOF (End-Of-File). For reasons associated with fundamental differences between tape and disk files, UCSD Pascal treats the interaction between EOF and GET, PUT, and SEEK in ways that differ significantly from the handling of EOF in Standard Pascal. Subsection 8.4.8 describes the handling of EOF in some detail because of its importance in controlling the other disk related statements.

As a final introductory note, RESET and CLOSE are automatically executed by UCSD Pascal for the predeclared files INPUT, OUTPUT, and KEYBOARD. Moreover, the definition of INPUT and OUTPUT files in UCSD Pascal differs from Standard Pascal because of fundamental differences in handling single-character transfers involving interactive terminals.

8.4.1 File Declarations and the Buffer (Window) Variable

If T is a predeclared or user-declared data type in a Pascal program, one declares a file identifier, for example FID, along with other variable declarations as in:

```
TYPE
  T=RECORD
      IFIELD:INTEGER;
      B:BOOLEAN;
      S:STRING;
    END;
VAR
  FID:FILE OF T;
  X,Y:INTEGER;
  A,B:T;
      .
      .
      .
```

The buffer variable associated with the file FID is referred to as FID↑. The up arrow or carat character should not be confused with the up arrow cursor positioning key on your keyboard. On some keyboards, the up arrow character used to qualify the file identifier so as to refer specifically to its buffer variable, may be a carat character. Assuming that RESET or REWRITE has previously been executed for this file, it is then possible to assign the value of the file's buffer variable, for example,

A := FID↑

or, if B has previously been assigned a set of values, then:

FID↑ :=B

Since the file is associated with a record type, it is also possible to assign individual fields from within the record as with any other record type variable. For example,

X :=FID↑ .IFIELD

or

FID↑ .IFIELD :=A.IFIELD

8.4.2 GET, PUT, READ, and WRITE

Assuming that the file FID has been declared as in Section 8.4.1, that the file is open, and that the position pointer of the indicated file points to a record actually stored on the disk, then:

GET(FID)

transfers one record from the disk file into the buffer variable FID . The record transferred is the one referred to by the position pointer. After the record is transferred, the position pointer associated with the file is advanced by one record position. Here again UCSD Pascal differs from Standard Pascal, in which GET advances the position pointer *before* transferring the record. The order is reversed in UCSD Pascal in order to make SEEK operate in a straightforward manner.

If the position pointer associated with the file points to a position not occupied by a record when GET(FID) is executed, then the End-Of-File flag associated with the file becomes set to true (see Section 8.4.8 regarding EOF), and the content FID↑ is left undefined. Experimentation with UCSD Pascal will show you that execution of GET(FID) with EOF already set to true, or when the position pointer points outside the range of record numbers contained in the file, will leave the content of FID↑ unchanged. This is not a behavior you should depend on, since Standard Pascal specifies that the contents of FID↑ are undefined under these conditions.

Assuming the declarations shown in Section 8.4.1, READ(FID,A) is equivalent to the following compound statement:

```
BEGIN
  A :=FID↑;
  GET(FID)
END
```

This definition is contained in the draft standard description of Pascal circulated for comments at the end of 1978. Previous definitions of Standard Pascal restricted the use of READ to text files. As a result, current versions of UCSD Pascal still do not support this use of READ for structured data files.

Again assuming that the file FID is open, and that the position pointer points to a legal record position, then the statement:

    PUT(FID)

transfers the current contents of the buffer variable FID↑ to that record position in the disk file. It then advances the position pointer to the next position. Once again, the transfer of data takes place in Standard Pascal *after* the position pointer is advanced.

In Standard Pascal, the only legal record position prior to execution of a PUT statement is the position just before the first unoccupied record position at the end of the file. In UCSD Pascal, because of the need to *update* any record in a disk file, the legal record positions include all positions starting with record zero, and extending to the highest numbered unused position following the current end of the file. Therefore, the condition of EOF(FID), before PUT(FID) is executed, has no effect on the PUT operation. If PUT transfers data to a record position located beyond the last currently occupied record in the file, ie: in an unused area immediately following the file and adjacent to it, then the disk directory will be updated to show that the file occupies all positions up to and including the position to which the transfer took place.

In UCSD Pascal, execution of PUT(FID) has no effect on the EOF(FID) flag unless it attempts to transfer data to an illegal record location, for example a location within a file which follows the open file to which PUT refers. In that case, EOF(FID) is set true, and no data transfer takes place. In versions of UCSD Pascal distributed before early 1979, execution of PUT(FID) when it refers to an illegal record location will also cause an input/output execution error. This will cause the program to terminate abnormally unless the Compiler's IOCHECK option has been turned off. If the program is expected to PUT data to all available unused positions, it will be necessary to use this option until the design error causing this abnormal termination can be corrected. See Section 8.7 on error recovery for further details.

Analogous to READ, the new draft description of Standard Pascal defines WRITE(FID,A) to mean:

    BEGIN
        FID↑:=A;
        PUT(FID)
    END

Again because older descriptions of Standard Pascal limited WRITE to operation with text files, UCSD Pascal does not yet allow use of WRITE with structured data files.

8.4.3 RESET, REWRITE, and CLOSE

As described in the introduction to Section 8.4, a program must inform the operating system *when* to allocate memory space to the block buffer for a disk file, and *which* file in the disk directory to equate with the internal file identifier. In the examples shown here, I will continue to use the internal file identifier FID, as declared in the example of Section 8.4.1, but of course any declared file identifier could be used. The program passes the necessary information to the operating system by executing a RESET or a REWRITE statement. After one of these statements is executed successfully, ie: without reporting an error, the file is then regarded as open and thus available to the program for input and output operations.

Unlike Standard Pascal, UCSD Pascal allows mixed input and output operations following either RESET or REWRITE. The new draft description of Standard Pascal states that if PUT(FID) is not separated from a previous GET(FID) or RESET(FID) by an intervening execution of REWRITE(FID), then the results to be expected from the PUT are implementation dependent. Since UCSD Pascal is designed to allow random access updating of disk files, it differs in several detailed respects from Standard Pascal regarding the opening and closing of disk files, and regarding the detection of end-of-file status (see Section 8.4.8).

8.4.4 RESET

To open a pre-existing disk file, ie: one with a directory entry already on the disk, use:

        RESET(FID, < title-string >)

where < title-string > may be either a quoted string or a string variable. Assuming that S is a variable of type STRING, either:

        RESET(FID, 'DATAFILE')

or:

        S := 'DATAFILE';
        RESET(FID,S)

would open a file with the directory title DATAFILE for use associated with the internal identifier FID. Notice that this arrangement allows the value of the string variable S to be assigned while the program is running, perhaps through use of a READ(S) statement which calls for the user of the program to type in the name of the file.

The string parameter which gives the file's directory title in a RESET statement is a nonstandard extension unique to UCSD Pascal. Both Standard Pascal and UCSD Pascal provide the form:

        RESET(FID)

In Standard Pascal, this is used to open the file, but the means of associating the file title with the internal identifier are left to be defined by the implementor (ie: the person or organization that arranges to install Pascal within a software system).

Once the file FID is open, both Standard Pascal and UCSD Pascal use RESET(FID) for the same basic purposes. The file's position pointer is moved back to the beginning of the file, and the contents of the first record stored in the file are assigned to the file's buffer variable. Although UCSD Pascal is oriented to disk files, this operation is like performing a rewind operation on a magnetic tape, and then executing a single (hidden) GET(FID) statement.

Either form of the RESET statement sets EOF(FID) = FALSE in UCSD Pascal, assuming that there is no error indication. An error will be indicated if RESET(FID, *filetitle*) cannot be completed because the requested *filetitle* cannot be found in the disk directory. The same form of RESET will also cause an error indication if FID is already open, since no indication will be available to the operating system at that point on what to do with the disk file that is already open. Repeated execution of RESET(FID) does not produce any error indication, since the only effect is to cause GET and PUT operations to start again at the beginning of the file. An error indication of either type mentioned here will cause your program to terminate abnormally unless you use a Compiler directive which suppresses I/O error terminations. This option is provided to allow the programmer to arrange for program recovery in the case of input or output errors. See Section 8.7 of this chapter for details.

8.4.5 REWRITE

To open a new disk file, one with a title not matched by an existing directory entry, use:

REWRITE(FID, < title-string >)

where the title string is required. Unlike RESET, REWRITE in UCSD Pascal has no optional form without a title string parameter. REWRITE in Standard Pascal uses no title string, and leaves optional the question of how the directory title will be established.

This statement requests the operating system to establish a new temporary directory entry for the file, and to allocate the block buffer area in memory needed for input and output operations. The directory entry will be made permanent as a result of executing a CLOSE(FID,LOCK) statement. Any file already on the disk with a directory title which matches the title string will be removed in order to make way for the new file. Vestiges of a directory entry for the new file will also remain on the disk after the REWRITE is executed, if you open the door of the floppy disk-drive and/or take the disk out of the machine. This is not an action that we advise, since the directory entry left on the disk in that way will probably not reflect accurately how many records have actually been PUT into the file. In fact, the directory will probably show that the file occupies the entire unused area to which it was allocated when the REWRITE was executed!

The form of the title string used with REWRITE will determine which un-used area on the disk the operating system will use in allocating space to the file. If you use a simple title string such as:

NEWFILE

then the file will be allocated starting at the beginning of the largest unused area currently in the directory. It will then be legal to execute PUT(FID) opera-tions referring to any record position throughout that (initially) unused area. The ultimate size of the file, as shown in the directory after the file is closed, will be the number of blocks starting at the beginning of the unused area, and extending through the highest numbered block to which a PUT(FID) operation is directed.

If you know in advance that the new file will not have to occupy more than a certain number of blocks, then an alternate form of title string may be useful. For example, if the number of blocks desired is no more than 15, then use the form:

NEWFILE[15]

Unfortunately, it is not possible to substitute a variable identifier for the desired number of blocks within this title string. However, the value actually passed to the REWRITE(FID,S) statement can be computed by the program, if the value of a STRING variable S is composed using the STRING operations provided in UCSD Pascal.

The operating system will respond to:

REWRITE(FID, 'NEWFILE[27]')

by allocating the file to the first unused area in the directory which contains at least 27 blocks. If no unused area at least 27 blocks long can be found, then an I/O error indication will result. In case of an error, the program will terminate abnormally unless the methods described in Section 8.7 of this chapter are used.

If you want to create two or more independent new files that are to be open-ed simultaneously, it will be necessary to use a strategy which, in effect, allows simultaneous creation of several temporary directory entries. One strategy would use REWRITE to request the space needed for the smallest file first. A SEEK to the last desired record position of that file should then be executed (see Section 8.4.7 for details), followed by PUT(FID) and then CLOSE(FID,LOCK) on the file. Then the same sequence can be repeated for the next larger file.

8.4.6 CLOSE

After the completion of a program's work in a disk file, it may be necessary to request the operating system to deallocate the block buffer area assigned to the file in memory. In the case of a new file opened with REWRITE, a permanent directory entry must be completed, if the file is to be retained. In the case of an established file opened with RESET, the directory may have to be updated to reflect the use of record positions that had previously been in the unused area adjacent to the file. In UCSD Pascal, these operations are accomplished in response to execution of a CLOSE statement, of which there are several forms. Standard Pascal provides no equivalent operation.

If the file has been opened with RESET, or if a new file opened with REWRITE is not to be retained, then use:

    CLOSE(FID)

If the file is new, having been opened using REWRITE, and you wish to retain the file with a permanent directory entry, then use:

    CLOSE(FID, LOCK)

If you wish to use a program to *remove* a disk directory entry with an effective equivalent of the R(emove command of the Filer, then open the file using:

    RESET(FID, < title-string>)

followed by:

    CLOSE(FID, PURGE)

All forms of CLOSE will mark the file FID no longer open. Further attempts to use GET, PUT, SEEK, EOF, READ, or WRITE referring to the file FID will result in an I/O execution error indication. Unless the method described in Section 8.7 is used, the program will then terminate abnormally. If a program terminates normally, without ever executing CLOSE for any file that is open at termination time, then the first illustrated form of CLOSE is automatically executed for each open file.

8.4.7 SEEK

To change the position pointer associated with an open file FID, use:

    SEEK(FID, < record-number>)

where the record number is an integer valued arithmetic expression. For example,

    SEEK(FID, 57);
    SEEK(FID, INTVAR);
    SEEK(FID, LASTREC - 2*I)

If the value of the record number is non-negative, then the next GET(FID) or

PUT(FID) to be executed will refer to the disk record indicated by that value. If the value of the record number is negative, then the result of the SEEK is undefined. (In Versions I.5, II.0, and II.1 of UCSD Pascal, SEEK with a negative record number will be executed but it has no effect.)

SEEK with a non-negative record number always sets EOF(FID) to false, regardless of whether the value of <record-number> is within the areas where GET or PUT operations would be legal. It is necessary to execute GET or PUT to discover whether EOF(FID) will remain false thus signifying successful completion of the GET or PUT. There is no equivalent of SEEK in Standard Pascal. At the time this book is being written (mid-1979), successive execution of SEEK without an intervening GET, PUT, EOF, or RESET referred to the same file may produce undefined results. Moreover, if <record-number> is large, the time taken for execution of SEEK may become excessive (several seconds). Both problems are under review, and SEEK may be improved in future versions of UCSD Pascal.

8.4.8 EOF

The built-in "End-Of-File" function:

EOF(FID)

is used to determine the result of an input or output operation. Because of a desire to keep UCSD Pascal extensions beyond Standard Pascal to a minimum, EOF works somewhat differently in UCSD Pascal than in Standard Pascal when dealing with a disk file. This makes it unnecessary to extend the language with another special function to handle virtually the same purpose for disk files alone.

If the disk file FID is already open, RESET(FID) will leave EOF(FID) set to false. If the disk file referred to by <title-string> is present in the disk directory, then RESET(FID, <title-string>) will leave EOF(FID) set to false. Otherwise, an I/O execution error will be indicated. If there is enough room to allocate space for the requested new file, REWRITE(FID, <title-string>) will leave EOF(FID) set to false. Otherwise, an I/O execution error indication will result. If the record position pointer associated with an open file FID points to any position starting with position zero, and ending with the last position containing a valid data record, then GET(FID) will leave EOF(FID) set to false. If the position pointer points to a location beyond the last valid data record, then GET(FID) will leave EOF(FID) set to true.

If the record position pointer associated with an open file FID points to any position already established within the file, or to any position within the unused area following the file, then PUT(FID) will leave EOF(FID) set to false. Otherwise, PUT(FID) will leave EOF(FID) set to true (and as UCSD Pascal is currently released, an I/O execution error will also be indicated). SEEK(FID, <record-number>) will leave EOF(FID) set to false if the value of <record-number> is non-negative. Otherwise the value of EOF(FID) will not be changed. If EOF(FID) is executed when the file FID is not open, it will return the value true.

8.4.9 Sample Program: Sequential File-to-File Copying

In this section we provide a simple concrete example of the use of the facilities just described for handling structured data files in UCSD Pascal. In this example, we copy the contents of one file into a new file on the disk. Both files are then left on the disk. Additional examples showing random access use of structured data disk files are shown in Section 8.5.

```
PROGRAM FILECOPY;
CONST RECSIZE=199;
TYPE
  STRUCTURE=
    PACKED ARRAY[0..RECSIZE] OF CHAR;
VAR
  RECNUM:INTEGER;
  FIN,FOUT:FILE OF STRUCTURE;
BEGIN
  RESET(FIN,'OLDFILE');
  REWRITE(FOUT,'NEWFILE');
  RECNUM:=0;
  WRITE('Copying');
  WHILE NOT EOF(FIN) DO
    BEGIN
      FOUT↑:=FIN↑;
      PUT(FOUT);
      RECNUM:=RECNUM+1;
      WRITE('.');
      GET(FIN);
    END;
  WRITELN;
  WRITELN(RECNUM, 'records copied');
  CLOSE(FOUT,LOCK);
END.
```

Listing 8.2 Sample program which copies from OLDFILE to NEWFILE.

In the simple example shown in listing 8.2, we ignore the internal layout of the fixed length records of type STRUCTURE. All we are concerned about is their total size, which is one more than the constant RECSIZE, or in this case 200 bytes. There is no information in the directory entry for a file indicating the structure of the records contained in the file. However, the directory does contain an integer value representing the number of the last record stored in the file. This number, multiplied by the size of the structured records originally PUT into the file, controls the value returned by EOF(FIN) following each use of GET(FIN). Thus, it is possible to refer to an old file by associating the input file type with a structure whose size is not the same as that used in creating the old file. However doing this will yield records not matched to those originally written into the file, and the EOF function will return TRUE for a GET when the position pointer does not point at the actual end of the file.

In this sample program, we assume that the file with the directory title OLDFILE exists on the disk before the program is run. A file called NEWFILE might also exist before the program is run, but that previous file will be removed as a result of the REWRITE statement in this program. If you want to avoid inadvertent loss of an old file in this way, it would be best to try to RESET the old file (ie: the existing file with the title NEWFILE) as a first step. Your program can then inform you if the RESET(FIN, < old-filename >) succeeds. If it does not, you will have to use the error recovery approach described in Section 8.7 of this chapter to avoid abnormal termination of your program. The program FILECOPY leaves its new copy in the file NEWFILE. This program displays two lines on the computer's console device, namely:

       Copying ....
       27 records copied

as direct verification for the user that the program is actually doing its work. The first line displays one dot after the PUT of the associated record is completed. The second line provides a simple summary. In general, you will probably find it useful to provide some visual indication of activity in any program that spends much time in disk I/O or other time consuming computations.

Notice that the GET takes place *after* the PUT within the main WHILE loop of the program. This is because the first GET effectively takes place as a part of the RESET statement referring to the input file FIN. The last executed GET statement switches the EOF(FIN) flag to true, and this information is immediately used to terminate the WHILE statement.

8.5 Random Access Handling of Disk Files

In this section, we will start with a disk file containing name, address, and telephone number information on some imaginary people. We will then illustrate how to go about updating selectively chosen records already in the file, and also appending additional records to the file.

In the example given here, we will assume that it makes sense to determine which record to select from the file by simply making use of its record number. In practical applications, this is obviously not a suitable procedure, and some means of indexing the records in the file must be used. The last subsection provides a brief discussion of indexing strategies, but no solid sample program example because of space limitations.

8.5.1 Sample Program UPDATE

The three parts of listing 8.3 show a sample program which illustrates the creation and updating of a simple file. Display 8.1 shows a portion of the screen display associated with this program. All of the disk file handling is accomplished in the main program, listing 8.3c. In a larger program containing indexed access to the stored records, management of available record positions and other amenities, the disk file handling statements should be isolated in procedures which can be readily altered without changing the whole program. This strategy reduces the amount of effort that may be necessary to change the program when moving from one machine to another with differing characteristics.

Handling of input from the keyboard and display on the screen is very simple in this sample program. In this program, the user is prompted to type-in the number of the record wanted. The current contents of the record are then displayed in a meaningful format. The user is then prompted to type in new contents for each field in the record separately. If the user wishes to leave a field unchanged, RETURN skips to the next field. ESC(ape followed by RETURN jumps out of the field updating cycle without any further change of a field. If the requested record position is in the unused area following the previous end of the file, the program prompts immediately for new contents.

```
(*$G+*)
PROGRAM UPDATE;
TYPE
  STRUCTURE=
  RECORD
    NAME,COMPANY:STRING[32];
    STREET:STRING[20];
    CITYSTATE:STRING[30];
    TEL:STRING[10]
  END;
VAR
  RECNUM:INTEGER;
  BUF:STRUCTURE;
  TITLE:STRING;
  FID:FILE OF STRUCTURE;

PROCEDURE ZEROREC(VAR REC:STRUCTURE);
BEGIN
  WITH REC DO
    BEGIN
      NAME:="";
      COMPANY:="";
      STREET:="";
      CITYSTATE:="";
      TEL:="";
    END;
END (*ZEROREC*);

PROCEDURE SHOWREC(REC:STRUCTURE);
BEGIN
  WRITELN;
  WITH REC DO
    BEGIN
```

```
              WRITELN('NAME:              ',NAME);
              WRITELN('COMPANY:           ',COMPANY);
              WRITELN('STREET:            ',STREET);
              WRITELN('CITY&STATE:        ',CITYSTATE);
              WRITELN('TELEPHONE:         ',TEL);
         END;
     END (*SHOWREC*);
```

Listing 8.3a: First part of sample program UPDATE.

```
  PROCEDURE GETREC(VAR REC:STRUCTURE);
  LABEL 1;
  VAR S:STRING;

    FUNCTION READIT(VAR T:STRING):BOOLEAN;
    BEGIN
      READLN(S);
      READIT:=FALSE;
      IF LENGTH(S)>0 THEN
        IF S[LENGTH(S)]=CHR(27(*ESC*)) THEN READIT:=TRUE
        ELSE
          T:=S;
    END (*READIT*);

  BEGIN
    WRITELN('RETURN skips item with no change;',
  ' ESC+RETURN skips whole Record');

    WRITELN;
    WITH REC DO
      BEGIN
        WRITE('NAME:              ');
          IF READIT(NAME) THEN GOTO 1;
        WRITE('COMPANY:           ');
          IF READIT(COMPANY) THEN GOTO 1;
        WRITE('STREET:            ');
          IF READIT(STREET) THEN GOTO 1;
        WRITE('CITY&STATE:        ');
          IF READIT(CITYSTATE) THEN GOTO 1;
        WRITE('TELEPHONE:         ');
          IF READIT(TEL) THEN GOTO 1;
      END;
```

Listing 8.3b: Second part of sample program UPDATE.

```
    1:
  END (*GETREC*);
```

```
BEGIN (*main program*)
  WRITE('File title:');
  READLN(TITLE);
(*$I-*)      (*turn off I/O error checking*)
  RESET(FID,TITLE);
  IF IORESULT<>0      THEN REWRITE(FID,TITLE);
(*$I+*)      (*turn on I/O checking again*)
  RECNUM:=0;
  WHILE RECNUM>=0 DO
    BEGIN
      WRITELN;
      WRITE('Record number:');
      READLN(RECNUM);
      IF RECNUM>=0 THEN
        BEGIN
          SEEK(FID,RECNUM);
          GET(FID);
          IF EOF(FID) THEN
            BEGIN
              WRITELN('Enter new Record:');
              ZEROREC(FID↑);
            END
          ELSE
            BEGIN
              WRITELN('Old Record:');
              SHOWREC(FID↑);
              WRITELN;
              WRITELN('Enter Changes:');
            END;
          GETREC(FID↑);
          SEEK(FID,RECNUM);
          PUT(FID);
        END;
    END (*WHILE*);
  CLOSE(FID,LOCK);
END.
```

Listing 8.3c: Third part of sample program UPDATE.

The Compiler directive (*$I—*) turns off the IOCHECK option so that the program can cope with the problem that may arise if the file whose directory name is read into TITLE happens not to be on the disk. In this simple program, the response to this is to create a new file using the REWRITE statement. The use of the IOCHECK option in connection with recovery from I/O errors is discussed in Section 8.7 of this chapter. If the IOCHECK option were not turned off, and the requested file not in the directory, then the RESET statement would cause the program to terminate abnormally.

```
Running
File title NAMEFILE

Record number 3
Old Record

NAME        Bull, Terry
COMPANY     Ramona Stock Farm
STREET      Box 48 RFD #2
CITY&STATE  Ramona, CA 92065
TELEPHONE   789-1573

Enter Changes
RETURN skips item with no change; ESC+RETURN skips whole Record

NAME
COMPANY
STREET
CITY&STATE Anytown, U S A█
```

Display 8.1: Illustration of display with UPDATE program.

The program cycles, each time requesting a new record number until a negative record number is typed in. It then terminates after closing the file with LOCK. If the file was already on the disk when the program started, the LOCK option would be ignored when the CLOSE statement was executed.

No provision is made for the problem which would occur if the requested record position were outside the existing file or unused area immediately following the file. In that case, this program will terminate abnormally. In addition, no provision is made for the case in which one simply wishes to read a record, and thus make no change at all in the record stored on the disk. In that situation, the PUT(FID) statement is not needed.

8.5.2 Indexed Access: Efficiency Considerations

While the design of data bases for use in the UCSD Pascal System is beyond the scope of this book, a few comments on efficiency and the construction of indexes may prove helpful.

In the terms relevant to this chapter, an index is a logical device which allows rapid determination of the position number of a record within a data file. The sequential index, which is one of the simplest data designs, is also one of the most useful in the interactive environment for which the UCSD Pascal System is designed. A sequential index is basically a table in which each entry is a record containing two fields:

● A copy of one field of a record from the main data file, for example the name of a person. This field is the *key* referred to by the index.

- The position number of the data record in the main data file which is associated with the value of the key in field (a).

The "table" might be stored, during processing, in an array of records containing these two fields. It is more likely to be stored on two levels, one (called the *coarse index*) in a small array, and the other (called the *fine index*) stored in a file. Because of space limitations, only one *page* of this file will be brought into the computer's memory at any one time (see below for a definition of *page*).

In any event, the records in the index table are sorted according to the value of the key, usually in ascending order. This makes it possible to use an efficient searching algorithm such as a binary search to find any entry having a specific key value in the index. In the interactive situation, one often knows only an approximate value for a desired key. One may not even know whether a given key is stored in the file and index. Either way, a binary search yields the location in the index where the key *would be located* if it were present. It is then possible to display a listing of a few index entries both before and after the one desired. A visual scan of this list will allow using a simple process to indicate whether the full data record associated with any particular index key value should be retrieved from the main data file. The record position number associated with the key in the index table entry is then used to make the desired random access to the data file. Many people refer to the use of a sequential index to make random access to a data file, as the *Indexed Sequential Access Method*, or simply ISAM, because of the widespread use of that term on the large IBM computers.

In a floppy disk-based interactive system, as in any other, there are questions about the design of the index, the order in which the data records of the main file should be stored, and many others. Typically the sequential index file is broken up into groups of several dozen to several hundred index table records, each group being stored in a separate large record in the index file. This makes it possible to bring a whole group of index table records into main memory in one GET operation. With a floppy disk file, the time required to complete one GET operation will be about 0.3 seconds on the more expensive machines, to more than one second on the more economical mini-floppy based machines. As a result, each group or *page* of index table entries should contain a reasonably large number of index entry records. If the number gets larger than can be accomodated in roughly half of one floppy disk track, then the time taken just to *transfer* the index page into memory becomes an important consideration.

If the size of the index is large enough to occupy several pages, a small coarse index should be maintained just to allow fast computation of the number of the index page in which a desired key value will be found. The time taken to perform a binary search within one index page will usually be far smaller than the time taken to access, ie: GET, just one index page from the disk. The entries in the coarse index usually contain copies of the last key value found in each page of the main index, which is now called the fine index. In floppy disk-based systems, the size of the coarse index will almost always be quite small. It therefore can be loaded into memory when the program is initialized, and maintained there without disk accesses until the files are closed.

If the sorted sequential index table is arranged to fill every available index record positon, then there will be serious problems in providing rapid interactive response to a user who is updating a file. Each update will probably require adding a new index record somewhere in the middle of the index, or deleting an old record from the middle. Even on large hard-disk based systems, the time taken to re-sort a sequential index is likely to be prohibitive. In some large systems, updates for a sequential index are kept temporarily in an overflow page. A search then requires looking both in the sorted area where the key is likely to be found, and in the overflow area. With floppy disks, the extra time needed to make access to both the main sorted area of the index, and also to the overflow area, may be prohibitive. In this case, an alternative strategy may be better. In this strategy, a portion of each index page is kept unused and available for expansion of the contents of the page. It then is only necessary to PUT the updated page containing the key when the update operation terminates.

Maintenance of the main data file will probably require occasional sorting at times when it is desired to conduct a *batch* (non-interactive) or bulk update operation involving a large fraction of all the data records in the file. Batch operations usually proceed sequentially from beginning to end of a file, rather than using randomly ordered accesses. The time needed to sort the main data file in a floppy disk system will probably run into many minutes, or even hours. However, the time saved in making it unnecessary to use an index in the batch update will often more than compensate for the time taken in the sort.

The data records are usually not moved during interactive updating activities. New records are appended to the end of the file, or they replace records that have been marked as *empty* during previous update transactions. Once it becomes necessary to sort the main data file, any indexes referring to that file must also be updated. The simplest and most efficient procedure will probably involve rebuilding the indexes after the sort is completed.

8.6 Text Files

Much of the input/output environment of Standard Pascal is designed for working with text files which can be thought of as stored on magnetic tape. UCSD Pascal provides two similar kinds of files for handling text streams of characters. A general description of text files in UCSD Pascal was given in Section 8.3 of this chapter. One kind, associated with the predeclared type TEXT, works essentially the same as type TEXT in Standard Pascal. The other, associated with type INTERACTIVE, is intended primarily for use with interactive terminal devices. However, both types can be used with disk files however. File variable declarations have the following appearance:

    FT:TEXT;
    FI:INTERACTIVE

Differences between these two forms are explained in the following sections.

8.6.1 READ and WRITE

The READ statement is used to obtain characters from the input device, and to assign value based on those characters to a variable within the program. If the variable is of type INTEGER or REAL, the value represented by the input stream of characters is converted into the internal binary form used by the program.

If CH is a variable of type CHAR, then

    READ(FT,CH)

is equivalent to:

    BEGIN
      CH :=FT↑;
      GET(FT)
    END

while:

    READ(FI,CH)

is equivalent to:

    BEGIN
      GET(FI);
      CH := FI↑
    END

In effect, a READ involving a variable of any other type causes repeated use of this form. If X is a variable of type INTEGER or of type REAL, then:

    READ(FT,X)

and:

    READ(FI,X)

carry out format conversion of the input character stream, and the internal binary form of the number is assigned to X. In either case, termination of the READ operation occurs upon detection of the first character which is not legally part of a constant of INTEGER or REAL type, as the case may be. In either case, the value of the window variable is left equal to the first non-numeric character following the number scanned by the READ statement. This is equivalent to including the first implicit GET(FI) operation of the *next*

READ(FI, . . .) at the end of READ(FI,X). Consequently, the next READ(FI, . . .) statement omits execution of the first implicit GET(FI). In this way, a sequence of READ(FI, . . .) or READ(FT, . . .) operations will produce the same values when reading the same disk file.

Note that RESET(FI, < title-string >) does not execute an implied GET(FI), whereas RESET(FT, < title-string >) executes GET(FT) automatically. If S is a variable of type STRING, then:

    READ(FT,S)   .

and:

    READ(FI,S)

both assign all characters from the input stream to S up to the next end-of-line character, or up to the maximum capacity of S. The end-of-line character is not moved into the string, and the file's character pointer is left pointing at the end-of-line character.

Output using:

    WRITE(FT,CH)

or:

    WRITE(FI,CH)

both produce the equivalent of:

```
BEGIN
  FT↑ := CH;
  PUT(FT)
END
```

In other words, output using WRITE gives the same results regardless of whether the file is declared to be of type INTERACTIVE or TEXT. If WRITE refers to a variable of type INTEGER or REAL, then format conversion takes place from internal binary form to an external stream of characters.

8.6.2 EOLN, READLN, WRITELN: End-Of-Line

Text files in Pascal are subdivided into lines, each consisting of a sequence of characters terminated by an end-of-line marker. In UCSD Pascal, the end-of-line marker is a single ASCII CR control character (carriage return) which has a decimal value of 13. In Standard Pascal, the end-of-line marker is not regarded as a character, and it cannot be handled in the way normal characters are handled. If you use conventional Pascal I/O operations with text files in

UCSD Pascal, you will have no occasion to work directly with the CR control character.

The built-in function EOLN (<file-identifier>) returns the value TRUE when the position pointer of a text file points at an end-of-line marker. This occurs at the termination of a READ statement which finishes its work because it encounters an end-of-line marker. Consider the program fragment shown in listing 8.4.

```
WRITELN;
RESET(FT);
WHILE NOT EOF(FT) DO
   BEGIN
      WHILE NOT EOLN(FT) DO
         BEGIN
            READ(FT,CH);
            WRITE(CH);
         END;
      READLN(FT);
      WRITELN:
   END;
```

Listing 8.4: Program fragment showing use of EOLN(FT).

The first WRITELN statement moves the video display cursor to the left margin of a new line. (Remember that READ or READLN, without an explicit reference to a file identifier, refer by default to the predeclared file INPUT, which in UCSD Pascal obtains characters from the keyboard. Similarly WRITE and WRITELN refer by default to the file OUTPUT.)

RESET(FT) leaves EOLN(FT) and EOF(FT) set to false. Individual characters from the first line in the file are then assigned to the character variable CH, and then written to the computer's console display device. READ(FT,CH) for the last text character on a line assigns that character to CH, and then executes the GET(FT) which picks up the end-of-line character. This leaves EOLN(FT) set to true, and the WHILE loop terminates.

READLN(FT) is equivalent to:

```
BEGIN
   WHILE NOT EOLN(FT) DO GET(FT);
   GET(FT);
END
```

which causes the file's position pointer to skip to the beginning of the next line of text. At the end of the WHILE statement in this fragment, the position pointer points to the end-of-line marker, the value returned by EOLN(FT) is set to true, and the contents of the window variable FT is a space character. The single GET(FT) then advances the pointer and picks up the first character on the next line. The matching WRITELN does the equivalent on the display in preparation for the next line of text.

To produce precisely the same result using a disk file FI declared to be of type INTERACTIVE, the program fragment in listing 8.5 should be used:

```
WRITELN;
RESET(FI);
WHILE NOT EOF(FI) DO
  BEGIN
    WHILE NOT EOLN(FI) DO
      BEGIN
        READ(FI,CH);
        IF NOT EOLN(FI) THEN
          WRITE(CH);
      END;
    READLN(FI);
    WRITELN;
  END;
```

Listing 8.5: Program fragment showing use of EOLN(FI).

The extra IF NOT EOLN(FI) . . . within the inner compound statement is needed to suppress writing the blank character assigned to CH by the last READ(FI,CH) on a line. If the program is only to be used for display purposes, there may be no reason to include the extra IF statement, since the display of this implied blank will usually not be noticed. If the program is to be used for copying one disk file into another, there may be no reason to use files of type INTERACTIVE, since WRITE statements function in the same manner for files of both type TEXT and type INTERACTIVE. Thus, the principal reason for using the program fragment shown in listing 8.4 would be a desire to use precisely the same program taking its input character stream either from a disk file or from the keyboard (by using the title string "CONSOLE:").

In order to account for the difference between handling of files of type INTERACTIVE, from those of type TEXT, READLN(FI) is equivalent to the fragment:

WHILE NOT EOLN(FI) DO GET(FI)

The trailing GET(FI) is not needed, as in the case of READLN(FT) since the next READ(FI, . . .) statement will implicitly perform a GET(FI) as its first action.

WRITELN(FT) is equivalent to WRITELN(FI), and both have the effect of appending an end-of-line marker to the output file.

8.6.3 Efficiency Considerations

For practical reasons associated with the way in which text files have been implemented in the UCSD Pascal System, it will generally cost much less processing time to READ into variables of type INTEGER, REAL, or STRING than to carry out the equivalent steps using repeated READ(CH) with associated program logic. The same general observation also applies to WRITE.

Note that it is often convenient in UCSD Pascal to fill a sequence of character positions with space characters using a statement like this:

WRITE(< output-file-identifier>,' ': <field-width>)

where <field-width> is an integer valued expression. This is compiled to be roughly the equivalent of:

FOR I: =1 TO <field-width> DO WRITE (<output-file-identifier>,' ')

and thus is much slower than:

WRITE(< output-file-identifier>, S: <field-width>)

where S is a variable of type STRING which has been preassigned a string of space characters.

If you plan to work with large text files in UCSD Pascal, you will probably find it useful to become acquainted with several built-in procedures and functions provided with the UCSD Pascal System expressly for working with packed arrays of characters (of which strings are a special case). These include MOVERIGHT, MOVELEFT, SCAN, and FILLCHAR. These are implemented so as to run about as fast as the host processor will support (usually in assembly language).

8.7 Error Recovery

Before you do much work with disk files, you will learn that I/O related processing errors do occur, and that it would be best to write programs capable of recovering from those errors without terminating abnormally. The potential sources of error are many. They include the following, as well as others not mentioned here:

- Marginal recording or playback error due to a flawed surface on the disk, or due to improper adjustment of the disk drive. This often will cause just a single isolated bit to be recovered by a program incorrectly. Most machines provide hardware intended to check for errors of this type. The operating system then rereads the data on input, and attempts to complete a GET operation without an error being signalled. The data thus obtained will usually be correct, but may contain an error in one or more bytes.
- Failure of a recording or playback operation with the result that a complete 512-byte block of data is unrecoverable (ie: for all practical purposes destroyed). This can happen as a result of having an intermittent electronic failure, or as a result of a power failure at the time when a PUT

operation is in progress.

- Failure of a READ statement due to encountering data of the wrong format. For example, a READ into an INTEGER variable will expect to find a space character, '+', '−', or a numeric digit. If the first character is a letter or special punctuation character, the READ statement will fail on a format I/O error.
- Loss of a complete disk for some reason. An example might be excessive temperature in the room where the disk is stored. Another might be failure of the disk drive mechanism.
- An attempt to PUT a record outside the disk area allocated to a file.
- An attempt to open a disk file that is not currently available on a disk drive (or volume) connected to the machine.
- An attempt to create a new disk file with a title that matches the title of a file already in the disk directory.

The UCSD Pascal System is programmed to terminate abnormally when an input/output related error is detected in a user program, unless the programmer has suppressed error termination logic using the Compiler directive (*$I − *). If this option is in use, then the programmer can determine whether each I/O statement has completed its work properly by checking the value of the built-in function IORESULT which returns an integer value. If the value of IORESULT is zero, then the most recent I/O related statement terminated normally, ie: with no error. Otherwise, the value of IORESULT is determined by the nature of the error, and it can be used to control whatever recovery action the programmer may wish to take. The values of IORESULT correspond to the I/O error messages given in Appendix D3 of this book.

Just how your program should proceed to cope with an error once it has been discovered is a large topic that I cannot discuss in more than a cursory way in this book. As a brief example, let us assume that you want to create a new disk file which is to occupy an area of 100 blocks. Since the disk may already contain other files, it is possible that there will be no unused area large enough to hold the file. A suitable recovery procedure for the user of your program might be to mount an alternative disk, which has previously been initialized with a UCSD Pascal file directory, but which is known to have enough space for the file. The program fragment shown in listing 8.6 shows how this might be handled.

```
(*$I − *)
REPEAT
  REWRITE(FID, 'VOLID:NEWFILE[100]');
  RSLT: = IORESULT;
  IF RSLT < >0 THEN
    IF RSLT = 8 THEN
      WRITELN('No room for file; Please mount another disk')
    ELSE
      IF RSLT = 9 THEN
        WRITELN('Requested volume is not on-line')
```

```
        ELSE
            WRITELN('Unable to open new file! Check disk drive');
    UNTIL RSLT=0;
    (*$I+*)
```

Listing 8.6: Program fragment illustrating use of IORESULT.

This program fragment is designed to loop until the REWRITE statement terminates normally. The user is given suggestions about how to cope with the most likely errors. The integer variable RSLT is needed to provide temporary storage for the value of IORESULT at termination of the REWRITE statement. Otherwise the WRITELN statement containing an error message will reset the value of IORESULT to zero, and the loop will terminate immediately whether there is an error or not!

In general, the IOCHECK option should be enabled again after any section of a program which requires it to be turned off in order to cope with specific errors. Otherwise the program may encounter an I/O error from which it cannot recover, yet it might continue to run causing further damage. To re-enable the IOCHECK option use the Compiler directive (*$I+*) as shown in listing 8.6.

As a general strategy for recovering from errors in working with disk files, you should generally arrange to save *backup* copies of master disk files periodically. How long the period is will depend upon how much work you are willing to do in recovering from an error which completely destroys the current working version of a file containing important data. To assist in backing up to an earlier version of your working file, it may be useful to retain a text file containing a copy of all input from the keyboard which resulted in updates to that file. It then should be possible to rerun the update program using the copied *audit trail* of input text from that file, and thus to recreate the state of the main data file as it was just before the fatal error took place.

9 Using Libraries of Specialized Routines (Units)

9.1 Goals for this Chapter

Once you have become an experienced beginner in the use of Pascal, you are likely to realize that it would be possible to extend the Pascal language to simplify the writing of programs in whatever field of applications you might happen to prefer. Rather than extending the language itself, it turns out to be better to provide sets of preprogrammed routines which perform frequently needed computations in various fields of applications. In the UCSD Pascal System, a set of preprogrammed routines can be grouped together in a separate *Unit* in such a way that any of the routines (procedures or functions) may be used as if they had been declared within the using Pascal program. Several Units may be grouped together into a disk file called a *Library*.

The main goal of this chapter is to provide an introduction showing how preprogrammed Units and Libraries can be *used* by Pascal programmers. Instructions on how to *prepare* a Unit to be used in this manner are beyond the scope of this book, but may be found in the main reference manual for the UCSD Pascal System. The introduction provided here is left rather general of necessity. Since dozens or even hundreds of preprogrammed Units for the UCSD Pascal System are likely to become available within the coming years, specific instructions on how to use each unit will have to be supplied along with the Units themselves in executable form.

9.2 The Reason for Having Preprogrammed Units

A principal reason for the growing popularity of Pascal is the fact that the language is powerful yet very concise. By "powerful" we mean that Pascal can be used with a minimum of effort to write programs in almost any field of applications, not to mention its use in writing system software. By "concise" we mean that the translation of Pascal programs into executable form requires a relatively small and relatively simple compiler compared with the compilers needed for COBOL, FORTRAN, PL/I, or similar general-purpose programming languages. Another principal strength of Pascal is that programs written in Pascal tend to be relatively "clean," ie: free of logical errors, compared to programs written in the other popular languages to perform the same actions.

Soon Pascal will almost certainly be given the status of a standardized programming language by the International Standards Organization. A growing community of programmers have come to realize that Professor Wirth's original design for Pascal provides a remarkable balance between conciseness and power. Programmers who have started to use Pascal for creating large and complex programs often have realized that the language lacks various specialized facilities that they know are built into COBOL, FORTRAN, PL/I or other high-level languages. They have then tried to bring about agreement with other programmers who want to use Pascal for similar purposes on how Pascal should be extended to provide the missing facilities. It has turned out to be virtually impossible to obtain any such agreement, because very few programmers agree on details of how the extensions should be designed. The only point on which agreement has been growing is that an international standard on Pascal is needed, and that it should be based almost entirely on Wirth's original definition of Pascal, with a few minor errors or misconceptions corrected.

In addition to interest in the conciseness and cleanness of Pascal, a large part of the Pascal user community has a strong interest in the *portability* of programs written in Pascal. In other words, they want a Pascal program written for one machine or software system to perform in the same way on another machine or software system. Typically, programs written in the older high-level languages BASIC and FORTRAN have lacked portability because each implementor has chosen to extend or alter these languages in the interest of making certain specialized tasks easier, and in the real or imagined interest of obtaining an advantage over commercial competitors. Even programs written in COBOL, which has the best long-term record of respect for the language standard, lack portability because of differences in the software systems within which the COBOL programs are to run. In effect, the language definition is always extended somewhat because of the input/output environment imposed by the software system provided with the host machine. The computer industry is still a long way from reaching agreement on standards for software systems. Thus, it has been inevitable that virtually every implementation of Pascal extends Wirth's definition for the base language, and some implementations also differ in detailed ways from his definition. Fortunately, the political process of obtaining agreement on an international standard definition for Pascal seems to be leading to a reduction in the differences from the base language.

The UCSD Pascal System has been designed to enhance the portability of application programs among many different small machines. This has been accomplished by arranging to run the same complete software system on all of these machines, thus avoiding the effective language differences imposed by the software. Unfortunately, the UCSD Pascal language differs slightly from the standard definition. In addition, UCSD Pascal contains several extensions that were found important in the early development of the UCSD Pascal Software System. Efforts are now in progress to revise the UCSD Pascal language in such a way as to improve its compatibility with a new international standard for Pascal.

With the understanding born of experience, the preprogrammed units facility, recently added to UCSD Pascal, now provides a way to extend the utility of the language through the use of a very small set of simple extensions to the standard base language. This facility now makes it possible to reduce the number of extensions contained in the UCSD Pascal *language*, while allowing the *utility* of UCSD Pascal to be greatly expanded.

9.3 Overview of Units

In UCSD Pascal, a Unit is a collection of procedures and/or functions which can be used as if they were declared within the using program. A Unit may also contain CONST, TYPE, and VAR declarations, and these may be used as if they were declared in the using program. A Unit is similar to an *Include file* (see Chapter 6, Section 6.4 of this book) in that the contents of the Unit are prepared separately from the text of the program in which it will be used. Unlike an Include file, a Unit is usually compiled separately from the using program. This makes it unnecessary to spend the time needed to compile the Unit each time it is used.

An Include file is just an ordinary text file, the contents of which are substituted by the Compiler for the directive:

(*$I include-file-name*)

Thus the Compiler must treat the entire contents of the Include file as if they were contained in the main source program file. If the Include file is long, then a large amount of compile time may be needed each time one compiles the program file containing the Include directive, even though the Include file may never be changed.

A Unit is prepared in two main sections, the INTERFACE section and the IMPLEMENTATION section. The INTERFACE section contains CONST, TYPE, and VAR declarations, as well as PROCEDURE and FUNCTION *heading* declarations. All of these declarations look just as they would if the same declarations were placed directly in the program which uses the Unit. All of the declarations in the INTERFACE section are intended to be treated as if they were actually present within the declarations at the global level of the program which uses the Unit. The IMPLEMENTATION section contains any LABEL declaration, and additional CONST, TYPE, VAR, PROCEDURE and FUNCTION declaration, along with the local declarations and executable parts of all the PROCEDUREs and FUNCTIONs.

The using program may refer only to the items contained in the INTER-FACE section. All of the contents of the IMPLEMENTATION are considered to be *private* to the Unit, and not available directly to the using program. The contents of the INTERFACE section are considered to be *public* and thus available directly to the using program.

During compilation of the using program, the contents of the INTERFACE section of a Unit are treated as if they were in an Include file referred to by an Include directive at the beginning of the using program. This allows the compiler to treat the public parts of a Unit just as if they had been included in the using program. Since the IMPLEMENTATION section of the Unit is precompiled, it does not need to be compiled again. In other words, the executable code part of the Unit needs to be generated by the Compiler only once, not each time the Unit is used. However, the routines (PROCEDUREs and FUNC-TIONs) whose headings appear in the INTERFACE section of the Unit may be called by the using program just as if their entire contents had been compiled along with the program.

The advantage of this approach is that a programmer can now be given a large library of routines designed to carry out most of the *primitive operations* commonly needed to write Pascal programs for almost any field of applications. For example, anyone who writes a program designed to display data on a terminal screen, or to collect input data by filling in the blanks in a form displayed on the screen, needs to perform certain simple operations over and over again. These operations may include placing the cursor at a particular location on the screen, clearing all parts of a line to the right of the cursor, clearing the entire screen from the cursor location to the end, underlining a specified field of columns on one line and accepting only certain data values within that field, and so on. A Screen-Control Unit providing routines for these and other purposes should be available for use with the UCSD Pascal System by the time this book is published. Moreover, different versions of this Unit will be available to cope with the different characteristics of various popular terminals, though the using programs will always refer to the same PROCEDURE and FUNCTION headings. To convert such a program for use with a new terminal, it will (usually) only be necessary to provide a Screen-Control Unit designed for that terminal.

As the UCSD Pascal System comes into widespread commercial use, it is expected that libraries of Units for a wide variety of purposes will become available through the vendors of the System itself. Since an experienced programmer will have little difficulty in preparing a Unit that others could use, it is likely that the vendors will offer a selection of Units to buyers, just as a book publisher offers a selection of books in the same field.

9.4 A Sample Unit and its Use

Listing 9.1 shows the INTERFACE section of a simplified Screen-Control Unit. Listing 9.2 shows a test program SCDEMO which uses this Unit. Whenever possible, arrangements will be made with commercial distributors of the UCSD Pascal System to include both the test program and the Unit with the files made available with the System. You should then be able to experiment with the program to verify your understanding of how Units work.

```
UNIT SCDEMO;
INTERFACE
TYPE
  SCCHSET = SET OF CHAR;
  SCKEYCOMMAND =
    (BACKSPACEKEY,ETXKEY,UPKEY,DOWNKEY,LEFTKEY,
    RIGHTKEY,NOTLEGAL);

VAR
  SCCH:CHAR;

PROCEDURE SCINITIALIZE;
PROCEDURE SCLEFT;
PROCEDURE SCRIGHT;
PROCEDURE SCUP;
PROCEDURE SCDOWN;
PROCEDURE SCGETCCH (VAR CH:CHAR;
                              RETURNONMATCH:SCCHSET);
FUNCTION   SCMAPCRTCOMMAND(KCH: CHAR):
                              SCKEYCOMMAND;

(*IMPLEMENTATION starts here*)

PROGRAM TESTSCUNIT;
(*$U SCDEMO.CODE*) (*use only if SCDEMO not in
                              SYSTEM.LIBRARY*)

USES SCDEMO;

VAR DONE:BOOLEAN;
    CH:CHAR;
    CHOK:SCCHSET;
PROCEDURE SQUAWK;
BEGIN
   WRITE(CHR(7(*BEL*) ) );
END;

PROCEDURE CONTROL(CMD:SCKEYCOMMAND);
BEGIN
```

```
IF CMD IN [BACKSPACEKEY, UPKEY, DOWNKEY, LEFTKEY,
                                   RIGHTKEY, ETXKEY] THEN
      CASE CMD OF
        BACKSPACEKEY:
          BEGIN
            SCLEFT;
            WRITE( ' ' );
            SCLEFT;
          END;
        LEFTKEY: SCLEFT;
        RIGHTKEY: SCRIGHT;
        UPKEY: SCUP;
        DOWNKEY: SCDOWN;
        ETXKEY: DONE: = TRUE
      END (*CASE*)
   ELSE
      SQUAWK;
END (*CONTROL*);

BEGIN (*MAIN PROGRAM*)
   SCINITIALIZE;
   CHOK: = [CHR(0)..CHR(31), 'A'..'Z'];
   WRITE
      ('Arrow keys move cursor; ETX terminates; BS erases visible
                                                          chars');
   DONE: = FALSE;
   REPEAT
      SCGETCCH(CH,CHOK);
      IF CH IN[CHR(0)..CHR(31)] THEN
         CONTROL(SCMAPCRTCOMMAND(CH) )
      ELSE
         WRITE(CH);
   UNTIL DONE;
END.
```

The program TESTSCUNIT makes use of the procedures and functions contained in the SCDEMO Unit. TESTSCUNIT also makes use of the scalar type SCKEYCOMMAND, and the variable SCCH, both of which are delcared in the INTERFACE section of the Unit.

For example, the first statement in the main section of the program TESTSCUNIT is a call to the procedure SCINITIALIZE which is contained in the Unit SCDEMO. Only the heading of the procedure appears in the INTERFACE section. In effect, the heading of the procedure here is like a FORWARD procedure declaration. The body of the procedure is declared in the IMPLEMENTATION section of the Unit, and its detailed contents are of no concern to us in working on the program. Of course one needs to know what each procedure in the Unit does in order to write the program sensibly. The SCINITIALIZE procedure is used to load initial values into tables used by the other procedures and function in the Unit.

The program TESTSCUNIT provides a means of moving the cursor about on the screen, and for typing uppercase letters wherever the cursor may be located. The BACKSPACE key (or its equivalent found in Appendix A or B) may be used to back over and erase a displayed character. Pressing the ETX key causes the program to terminate. Cursor movement is controlled by the procedures SCUP, SCDOWN, SCRIGHT, and SCLEFT, all of which are contained in the Unit.

The procedure SCGETCCH is used to read one character (a command character) from the keyboard, returning the value of that character in the variable parameter CH. The procedure fails to return if a character typed on the keybaord is not in the set RETURNONMATCH. Instead, additional characters are read from the keyboard until a character falling in that set is pressed. In the main program of TESTSCUNIT, the variable CHOK is initialized to the set of characters considered "OK" when SCGETCCH is called within the REPEAT loop.

If the character returned by SCGETCCH falls in the group of control characters, which in ASCII code have decimal equivalent values ranging from 0 to 31, then the procedure CONTROL is called. The single parameter of CONTROL is of type SCKEYCOMMAND, which is the scalar type declared in the Unit. But the values returned by SCGETCCH correspond to the codes assigned to the keys on your keyboard. Since there are no industry standards on which character codes should be associated with the cursor positioning arrows (up, down, right, left), it is necessary to arrange for the arrow keys to cause the corresponding display procedures to be called. This is accomplished with the help of the function SCMAPCRTCOMMAND which accepts a character value as its input parameter, and returns a value of type SCKEYCOMMAND. This function makes use of a table hidden in the Unit which relates each ASCII control code to one value of type SCKEYCOMMAND. The values in the table are initialized by the procedure SCINITIALIZE, often by reading information stored in the miscellaneous information file supplied with the UCSD Pascal System. The program SETUP, also supplied with the System, can be used to alter the miscellaneous information file if you have a video terminal other than those for which the System is commonly supplied.

You might ask why we do not simply arrange to have the arrow keys move the cursor on the screen without having to handle the problem explicitly in a Pascal program. The reason is that many programs are written to control the response to cursor movement key commands in different ways depending upon circumstances. For example, in the Editor's I(nsert command, use of the arrow keys could cause a mess on the screen if they were not trapped out and translated into the question-mark character ("?"). However, outside the I(nsert command, the Editor makes use of the arrow keys to move the cursor in the familiar way.

Notice the two lines immediately following the program's heading line, ie:

```
PROGRAM TESTSCUNIT;
(*$U SCDEMO.CODE*)
USES SCDEMO;
```

The Unit is made available to the program by the USES statement, which must appear immediately following the PROGRAM heading, before any of the program's own declarations. The comment line contains an optional compiler directive which informs the Compiler which disk file to reference for any subsequent Units referred to by the USES statement. If all the Units you wish to employ are in the file SYSTEM.LIBRARY, then there is no need to employ the directive:

```
(*$U library-filename*)
```

since the Compiler assumes that all Units referred to in the USES list are to be found in SYSTEM.LIBRARY unless told otherwise. If you want to use Units called UNITA and UNITB, both located in the SYSTEM.LIBRARY, and also the Unit SCDEMO as above, then the USES statement should read as follows:

```
USES UNITA,UNITB,
(*$U SCDEMO.CODE*)
    SCDEMO;
```

If Units from several different files are to be used, then place the appropriate Compiler directive referring to each file before the list of Units contained in that file in the USES statement. The program may contain only one USES statement.

9.5 Linker Complications

In versions I.5, II.0, and III.0 of the UCSD Pascal System, which were released earlier than version II.1, it is necessary to use the Linker to bind together a program and the separately compiled Units that the program USES. Beginning with version II.1, *Intrinsic Units* have become available, and do not require the use of the Linker.

To explain the possible confusion about the version numbers, version III.0 differs from II.0 primarily by providing facilities for executing two or more procedures concurrently. This feature was necessary to make practical the Western Digital Microengine (a trademark of Western Digital), and other possible microprocesor implementations of UCSD Pascal, since there is no other means of writing interrupt input/output routines. Intrinsic Units require modifications to both II.0 and III.0 versions, and hence II.1 is a later version than both II.0 and III.0.

Version II.1 requires that all Intrinsic Units be in the library file called SYSTEM.LIBRARY. Later version will relax this restriction.

If you have a version of the System which provides Intrinsic Units, then you can probably ignore the rest of this section. If your version of the System requires the Linker for all Units referred to by a USES statement in a program, then the following notes should help. More detailed information on the Linker is contained in the main Reference Manual on the UCSD Pascal System.

If all Units you wish to use are contained in the file SYSTEM.LIBRARY, then the Linker is automatically executed the first time you use the R(un command following an E(dit change in your program file. The Linker is not executed immediately if you use the C(ompile command after editing changes. After a successful compilation, the next R(un command will invoke the Linker if necessary to complete the linking of the Units used by the program.

You can execute the Linker independently of the R(un command by using the L(ink command in the main "Command:" world of the System. It is necessary to do this when your program uses Units from files other than the SYSTEM.LIBRARY. Figure 9.1 shows the interaction with the Linker needed to bind together the compiled code file SYSTEM.WRK.CODE with the code file of the Unit SCDEMO to obtain a complete program code file TESTSCUNIT.CODE. In this figure, input sequences typed by the user are shown *underlined*. <RET> indicates pressing of the RETURN key.

```
Linker [II.0]
Host file? SYSTEM.WRK.CODE<RET>
Opening SYSTEM.WRK.CODE
Lib file? SCDEMO.CODE <RET>
Opening SCDEMO.CODE
Lib file? <RET>
Map name? <RET>
Reading TESTSCUN
Output file? TESTSCUNIT.CODE
Linking SCDEMO #10
Linking TESTSCUN #1
```

Figure 9.1: Interaction with the linker.

The host file is the program code file generated by the Compiler from your program text file. In Figure 9.1, the reserved file name of workfile is used.

The legend "Lib file?" requests the name of a library file containing Units that are to be linked. A simple <RET> rather than the name of a file tells the Linker that no more library files are to be linked. "Map name?" can be the name of a file into which a detailed directory of the linked data items and routines will be written. In the example of Figure 9.1, <RET> tells the Linker not to bother with generation of the directory file.

The "Output file?" is the name of the executable code file to be linked together from the code file generated by the Compiler, and all of the Units used by the program in that code file. Be sure to use a ".CODE" suffix in this name so that the resulting file may be executed.

The final lines with the legend "Linking" list the segment numbers attached to each of the Units linked, as well as the main program itself. These segment numbers may be useful in finding the source of an abnormal program termination due to an execution error, as described in Section 6.8 of Chapter 6. In general, you will not have access to the Pascal source program text file of a Unit, and will have to refer the problem to the supplier of the Unit if an execution error occurs in a Unit.

9.6 The Librarian

A utility *Librarian* program file called LIBRARY.CODE is supplied with the UCSD Pascal System for the purpose of binding together various separately compiled Units into a single library file. As this book was going to press, the rules for using this program were changing to accomodate the new Intrinsic Units. As a result, we are unable to give detailed instructions on use of the Librarian in this book. Details will be issued for distribution to users when they are available.

In general, a beginning user of the UCSD Pascal System should expect to obtain a complete set of Units bound together into a library file by anyone who sells/provides that user with a copy of the UCSD Pascal System. This should make it unnecessary to employ the Librarian program until the user has developed a reasonable level of sophistication in use of the UCSD Pascal System. A user who wishes to join separately prepared Units into an existing library file will have to use the Librarian to do so. The main Reference Manual for the UCSD Pascal System, or updates thereto, will be the best source of information on using the Librarian for the version of the System you are using.

APPENDIX A1
Apple II™ Computer

Machine Configuration

The Apple II (trademark of Apple Computer Inc.) requires an add-on memory board from Apple Computer, called the Language Card, to use the UCSD Pascal System, 48 K programmable memory bytes, and at least one floppy disk drive. Follow installation instructions supplied by APPLE Computer.

The standard Apple II television display can display only 40 columns of text. Nevertheless, the UCSD Pascal System treats the Apple II display as if it were a full 80 columns wide. At any instant, you can see only 40 of the 80 columns. Press Control + A to see either the left half or the right half of the logical 80-column screen. Press Control + A again to see the *other* half. In some contexts, you can cause the display to shift horizontally in such a way as to keep the cursor on the screen by pressing Control + Z.

Disk Notes

Assuming that the disk interface card is in slot 6, PORT 1 of the Apple II disk interface is logical Unit #4 in the UCSD Pascal System. PORT 2 is logical Unit #5. When the power is on, the computer looks for a disk containing the UCSD Pascal Interpreter file (SYSTEM.APPLE) on Unit #4. As the System is initially supplied by Apple Computer either the disk marked "APPLE1:" or the disk marked "APPLE3:" can be in Unit #4.

If you have just one disk drive, the disk marked "APPLE0:" should be substituted for "APPLE1:" or "APPLE3:" after the powerup bootstrap loading sequence completes its work. Press RESET to get the System to reinitialize itself so that you can use "APPLE0:" for program development. With a two-drive Apple II configuration, "APPLE1:" is normally in logical Unit #4, "APPLE2:" is normally in Unit #5.

The standard Apple II configuration uses 5-¼ inch floppy disks of either the hard-sectored or soft-sectored styles (the Apple II ignores the sector tracking hole). Blank disks must be formated using a program called FORMATTER which is supplied with the System. Each disk has a capacity for 280 of the 512-byte blocks used with the UCSD Pascal file system.

Special Keyboard Keys

To get	Press
ESC	ESC
DEL	CTRL+X
RET	RET
EOF	CTRL+C
backspace	← (left arrow key)
ETX	CTRL+C
TAB	CTRL+I
Break	Reset, forces System to re-initialize!
down arrow	CTRL+L
up arrow	CTRL+O
left arrow	← (left arrow key)
right arrow	→ (right arrow key)
]	shift+M
[	CTRL+K
LF	CTRL+J
Stop	CTRL+S, stops display of text until pressed again
DC1	CTRL+Q, in Editor's I(nsert jumps to left margin
screen swap	CTRL+A, 40 spaces at a time, turns off auto-follow
auto-follow	CTRL+Z, displayed 40 columns follow the cursor
Flush	CTRL+F, discards output waiting to be displayed

APPENDIX A2
TRS-80™ Computer

Machine Configuration

To use the UCSD Pascal System with the TRS-80 (trademark of Radio Shack Corporation) you need the TRS-80 Expansion Interface unit with a total of at least 48 K bytes of memory. Practical use of the System really requires two of the Mini-Disk drives.

Software Notes

The UCSD Pascal System for the TRS-80 is distributed under license by FMG, a subsidiary of Applied Data Corporation, 5280 Trail Lake Drive, Suite 14, Forth Worth, Texas 76133. Details on how to bootstrap load the System, and an operating UCSD Pascal with the TRS-80 are supplied by them with the software.

Special Keyboard Keys

Since the TRS-80 has no CONTROL key, it must be simulated by pressing the SHIFT key simultaneously with the down arrow, which are adjacent on the left side of the keyboard. This combination is shown as CTRL/DA in the following table.

To get	Press
ESC	Break key
DEL	CTRL/DA+U
RET	ENTER
EOF	CTRL/DA+C
backspace	← (left arrow key)
ETX	CTRL/DA+C
TAB	CTRL/DA+I
Break	CTRL/DA+B
down arrow	↓ (down arrow key)
up arrow	↑ (up arrow key)
left arrow	← (left arrow key)
right arrow	→ (right arrow key)
]	shift+right arrow
[	shift+left arrow
LF	↓ (down arrow key)
Stop	CTRL/DA+@, stops display until pressed again
DC1	CTRL/DA+Q, Editor's I(nsert jumps to left margin
Flush	CTRL/DA+F, discards output waiting for display

APPENDIX A3
Terak 8510a™ Computer

Machine Configuration

The 8510a is a product of Terak Corporation (Terak is their trademark), 14405 North Scottsdale Road, Scottsdale, Arizona 85260. The 8510a is built around the Digital Equipment Corporation LSI-11 processor. It is widely used together with the UCSD Pascal System by educational institutions which are members of EDUCOM, a nonprofit consortium of universities and colleges.

Disk Drive Numbers

#5 (optional

Terak   8512   QX1

on/off/bootstrap switch

#4

Terak   8510   QX0

Disks are inserted into the drives with the label closest to you and facing toward the ceiling. Push the disk all the way and close the door. The 8510a uses 8-inch diameter soft-sectored floppy disks compatible with the IBM 3740 diskette.

Disks will eject automatically upon opening the drive door either by directly opening the door or using the open button, newer models have this feature.

Special Keyboard Keys

To get	Press
ESC	ESC
DEL	DEL
RET	RET
EOF	ETX
BS	BS
ETX	ETX
Break	CTRL+9 (numeric pad)
down arrow	↓ (down arrow key)
up arrow	↑ (up arrow key)
left arrow	← (left arrow key)
right arrow	→ (right arrow key)
LF	linefeed key or CTRL+J
TAB	TAB or CTRL+I
DC1	DC1, in Editor's I(nsert jumps to left margin
Alpha	DC2, Upper/Lowercase toggle
Stop	DC3, or CTRL+S
Flush	CTRL+F

APPENDIX B1
ADM3-A™ Terminal

Special Keyboard Keys

To get	Press
ESC	ESC
RET	RETURN
DEL	RUBOUT
EOF	CTRL+C
backspace	left arrow key
TAB	CTRL+I
ETX	CTRL+C
Break	CTRL+B
down arrow	↓ (down arrow key)
up arrow	↑ (up arrow key)
left arrow	← (left arrow key)
right arrow	→ (right arrow key)
Stop	CTRL+S
Flush	CTRL+F

Notes:
  a) ADM3-A is a trademark of Lear Siegler Inc.

b) The key assignments shown here are suggested by the UCSD Pascal Project, but not required. Because it is easy to change these assignments using the SETUP program, some vendors may use other key assignments.

APPENDIX B2
Hazeltine 1500 Terminal

Special Keyboard Keys

To get	Press
ESC	ESC
RET	RETURN
DEL	Shift+DEL
EOF	CTRL+C
Backspace	BACKSPACE
TAB	TAB
ETX	CTRL+C
Break	BREAK or CTRL+@
down arrow	CTRL+K
up arrow	CTRL+L
left arrow	BACKSPACE
right arrow	CTRL+P
Stop	CTRL+S
Flush	CTRL+F

Notes: The key assignments shown here are suggested by the UCSD Pascal Project, but not required. Because it is easy to change these assignments using the SETUP program, some vendors may use other key assignments.

APPENDIX B3
Soroc IQ 120 Terminal

Special Keyboard Keys

To get	Press
ESC	ESC
RET	RETURN
DEL	RUBOUT
EOF	CTRL+C
Backspace	left arrow key
TAB	TAB
ETX	CTRL+C
Break	BREAK
down arrow	(down arrow key) ↓
up arrow	(up arrow key) ↑
left arrow	(left arrow key) ←
right arrow	(right arrow key) →
Stop	CTRL+S
Flush	CTRL+F

Notes: The key assignments shown here are suggested by the UCSD Pascal Project, but not required. Because it is easy to change these assignments using the SETUP program, some vendors may use other key assignments.

APPENDIX B4
Adapting the UCSD Pascal System to Your Video Display

When the UCSD Pascal System is bootstrap loaded, it loads the contents of a file called SYSTEM.MISCINFO into memory. SYSTEM.MISCINFO contains a table of information which includes the character codes commonly used with video terminals. Many of the distributors of the UCSD Pascal System are now including separate files corresponding to popular terminals. If one of these files corresponds to your terminal, it should be used in place of the SYSTEM.MISCINFO file supplied with the System. The titles of these separate files usually bear an obvious relationship to the name of the terminal and to MISCINFO. For example:

SOROC.MISCINFO

If you can use the Filer at all, even if the displayed information is not exactly like that shown in the figures in Chapter 5 of this book, you can change the directory name of the MISCINFO file for your terminal to SYSTEM.MISCINFO. For backup purposes, you would be well advised to change the name of the SYSTEM.MISCINFO file initially supplied to you to another name.

If there is no MISCINFO file for your terminal with your copy of the UCSD Pascal System, you probably can adapt the System to your terminal using the program SETUP. The file SETUP.CODE should be on one of your disks. SETUP allows you to change the video display and associated keyboard con-

trol codes in the memory table initialized from the SYSTEM.MISCINFO file.
The following sequence should be used:

- eX(excute SETUP (from the "Command:" world).
- Use the C(hange option of Setup.
- Use the P(rompted option of Change.
- Bypass each item you wish to leave unchanged by pressing N(o.
- For each item you wish to change, press Y (for Y(es) The program will prompt for a new value, which by default should be entered as a decimal number. The program will again prompt and ask whether you want to change the same item. If not, continue by pressing N.
- When you have examined or changed all the desired items, you can jump out of the loop by pressing "!" (exclamation point). Press Q for Q(uit twice to reach the "Quit:" world of this program. The D(isk option will leave a file called NEW.MISCINFO on the disk. To use this new file, change its name to SYSTEM. MISCINFO and then bootload the System again.

In addition to changing the SYSTEM.MISCINFO file, adaptation of a new terminal to current versions of the UCSD Pascal System usually requires changing an internal procedure of the operating system which handles the built-in GOTOXY procedure. This must be accomplished by separately compiling a substitute GOTOXY procedure designed for use with your terminal. The new procedure must then be bound into the operating system using a program called BINDER, which is also supplied with the System software. The process of making this change is not difficult, but does require some caution. We suggest that you enlist the help of someone with experience in the use of the UCSD Pascal System to make this change. Further details are available in the main Reference Manual for the UCSD Pascal System.

APPENDIX C1
Screen Editor Commands

<repeat factor> is a number typed before any of the following commands. If not typed at all, value of <repeat factor> is assumed to be 1. "/" in place of a number causes repetition until the end of the file is reached.

<direction> is either forward or backward. Current <direction> is indicated by the broken bracket in 1st character position of the prompt line. ">" signifies foward. "<" signifies backward. Press ">" key to force direction to be forward, or "<" to force backward.

<down-arrow>	moves <repeat-factor> lines down
<up-arrow>	moves <repeat-factor> lines up
<right-arrow>	moves <repeat-factor> spaces right
<left-arrow>	moves <repeat-factor> spaces left
<space>	moves <repeat-factor> spaces in <direction>
<back-space>	moves <repeat-factor> spaces left
<tab>	moves <repeat-factor> tab positions in <direction>
<return>	moves to the beginning of line <repeat-factor> lines in indicated <direction>
"<" "," "-"	changes indicated <direction> to backward
">" "." "+"	changes indicated <direction> to forward

"="   moves to the beginning of what was just found, replaced, inserted, or exchanged

A(djust: Adjusts the indentation of the line that the cursor is on. Use the arrow keys to move. Moving up or down adjusts line above or below by same amount of adjustment as on the line you were on. < repeat-factor> is valid. < ETX> terminates.

C(opy: Buffer - Copies what was last inserted, deleted, or zapped into the file at the position of the cursor.

     File - Copies from a portion of all of a text file that exists in the directory. Partial files are identified by use of file markers.

D(elete: Treats the starting position of the cursor as the anchor. Use any moving commands to move the cursor. < ETX> deletes everything between the cursor and the anchor. < ESC> cancels the deletion.

F(ind: Operates in Literal or Token mode. Finds the < target> string. Use any special character to delimit the < target>. < repeat-factor> is valid. < direction is applied. "S" may be substituted for the < target> previously used.

I(nsert: Inserts text. Use < Backspace> to erase one inserted character, < DEL> erases last inserted whole line. < ETX> accepts inserted text. < ESC> cancels the insertion.

     J(ump: Jumps to the B(eginning, E(nd, or previously set marker.

M(argin: Adjusts anything between two blank or command lines to the margins which have been S(et in the E(nvironment. Command lines are identified by "↑" in 1st column. Invalidates the copy buffer.

P(age: Moves the cursor one page in indicated < direction>. < repeat-factor> is valid. < direction> is applied.

Q(uit: Leaves the editor. You may U(pdate, E(xit, W(rite, or R(eturn.

R(eplace: Extension of the F(ind command. Operates in L(iteral or T(oken mode. Replaces the < target> string with the < substitute> string. V(erify option asks you to indicate whether each occurrence of the < target> is to be replaced or skipped. "S" may substitute for either < target> or < substitute> and means that previous < target> or < substitute> is to be used < repeat factor> applies. < direction> is valid.

     < ESC> aborts R(eplace before specifications are complete.

S(et: M(arkers by assigning a string name to them.
    E(nvironment for:
        A(uto-indent, F(illing, M(argins, T(oken, and C(ommand characters.

V(erify: Redisplays the screen with the cursor in center of screen.

eX(change: Exchanges the current text for the text typed while in this mode. Each line must be done separately. <back-space> causes the original character to re-appear. <ETX> completes the exchange.

Z(ap: Treats the starting position of the last thing found, replaced, or inserted as an anchor and deletes everything between the anchor and the current cursor position.

APPENDIX C2
File Manager Commands

<wild> indicates wildcards can be used. "=" substitutes for all or part of
each file name, and cuases automatic reference to all files matching
the resulting pattern. "?" is similar to "=" but requests the user to
indicate whether each individual file should be affected by the command.

B(ad blocks: Scans the disk and detects bad blocks.

C(hange: Changes a file or volume name. <wild>

D(ate: Lists the current system-disk date, and enables the user to change all or
part of that date.

E(xtended list: Lists the specified directory as in L(dir but in more detail.
<wild>

G(et: Loads the designated file into the workfile.

K(runch: Moves the files on the specified volume so that all the unused blocks
are moved to the end of the disk.

L(dir: List a specified disk's directory or any subset thereof to the volume and

file specified ("CONSOLE:" is default).
<wild>

M(ake: Creates a directory entry with the specified name and size.

N(ew: Clears the workfile (workspace).

P(refix: Changes the current default volume identifier to the volume specified.

Q(uit: Returns user to the "Command:" world.

R(emove: Removes file entries from the specified directory. <wild>

S(ave: Saves the workfile under the name specified by the user.

T(ransfer: Copies the specified file(s) to the given destination. <wild>

W(hat: Identifies the name and state (saved or not saved) of the workfile.

V(olumes: Lists volumes currently on-line, along with their unit numbers.

eX(amine: Attempts to physically repair suspected bad blocks.

Z(ero: Creates a blank directory on the specified volume. The previous directory is no longer retrievable. Creates a directory on previously uninitialized disks (but does not *format* a previously unformatted disk).

APPENDIX C3
Operating System Commands

A(ssem: Executes the Assembler (SYSTEM.ASSEMBLER). The Assembler expects its input in SYSTEM.WRK.TEXT and generates its output in SYSTEM.WRK.CODE.

C(omp: Executes the Pascal Compiler (SYSTEM.COMPILER).

D(ebug: This is a hook intended to execute a user program under control of the system debugger. As this book went to press, the debugger still needed too much debugging to be released, and it probably will not be in your copy of the System.

E(dit: Executes the Screen Editor (SYSTEM.EDITOR).

F(ile: Executes the File Manager (SYSTEM.FILER).

H(alt: Stops execution of the Pascal P-machine Interpreter. The System must be bootloaded to restart.

I(nit: Re-initializes the System.

L(ink: Executes the System's Linker program, used for linking together separately compiled Units, and Segment procedures, with a user's main host program.

U(ser: Re-starts the program which most recently was executed.

eX)ecute: Prompts for the name of a CODE file for a program to be executed. If that name (leaving off the ".CODE") is typed in, and terminated with RETURN, and the name is found in the disk directory, then the named program will be exectued.

APPENDIX D1
Compiler Syntax
Error Messages

1 : Error in simple type
2 : Identifier expected
3 : 'PROGRAM' expected
4 : ')' expected
5 : ':' expected
6 : Illegal symbol
7 : Error in parameter list
8 : 'OF' expected
9 : '(' expected
1 0 :Error in type
1 1 :'[' expected
1 2 :']' expected
1 3 :'END' expected
1 4 :';' expected
1 5 :Integer expected
1 6 :'=' expected
1 7 :'BEGIN' expected
1 8 :Error in declaration part
1 9 :error in <field-list>
2 0 : '.' expected
2 1 : '*' expected
2 2 : 'Interface' expected

2 3 : 'Implementation' expected
2 4 : 'Unit' expected

5 0 : Error in constant
5 1 : ': =' expected
5 2 : 'THEN' expected
5 3 : 'UNTIL' expected
5 4 : 'DO' expected
5 5 : 'TO' or 'DOWNTO' expected in for statement
5 6 : 'IF' expected
5 7 : 'FILE' expected
5 8 : Error in <factor> (bad expression)
5 9 : Error in variable

101: Identifier declared twice
102: Low bound exceeds high bound
103: Identifier is not of the appropriate class
104: Undeclared identifier
105: sign not allowed
106: Number expected
107: Incompatible subrange types
108: File not allowed here
109: Type must not be real
110: <tagfield> type must be scalar or subrange
111: Incompatible with <tagfield> part
112: Index type must not be real
113: Index type must be a scalar or a subrange
114: Base type must not be real
115: Base type must be a scalar or a subrange
116: Error in type of standard procedure parameter
117: Unsatisified forward reference
118: Forward reference type identifier in variable declaration
119: Re-specified params not OK for a forward declared procedure
120: Function result type must be scalar, subrange or pointer
121: File value parameter not allowed
122: A forward declared function's result type can't be re-specified
123: Missing result type in function declaration
124: F-format for reals only
125: Error in type of standard procedure parameter
126: Number of parameters does not agree with declaration
127: Illegal parameter substitution
128: Result type does not agree with declaration
129: Type conflict of operands
130: Expression is not of set type
131: Tests on equality allowed only
132: Strict inclusion not allowed

133: File comparison not allowed
134: Illegal type of operand(s)
135: Type of operand must be boolean
136: Set element type is not compatible with the declaration
137: Set element types must be compatible
138: Type of variable is not array
139: Index type is not compatible with the declaration
140: Type of variable is not record
141: Type of variable must be file or pointer
142: Illegal parameter solution
143: Illegal type of loop control variable
144: Illegal type of expression
145: Type conflict
146: Assignment of files not allowed
147: Label type incompatible with selecting expression
148: Subrange bounds must be scalar
149: Index type must be integer
150: Assignment to standard function is not allowed
151: Assignment to formal function is not allowed
152: No such field in this record
153: Type error in read
154: Actual parameter must be a variable
155: Control variable cannot be formal or non-local
156: Multidefined case label
157: Too many cases in case statement
158: No such variant in this record
159: Real or string tagfields not allowed
160: Previous declaration was not forward
161: Again forward declared
162: Parameter size must be constant
163: Missing variant in declaration
164: Substitution of standard proc/func not allowed
165: Multidefined label
166: Multideclared label
167: Undeclared label
168: Undefined label
169: Error in base set
170: Value parameter expected
171: Standard file was re-declared
172: Undeclared external file
174: Pascal function or procedure expected
182: Nested units not allowed
183: External declaration not allowed at this nesting level
184: External declaration not allowed in interface section
185: Segment declaration not allowed in unit
186: Labels not allowed in interface section

187: Attempt to open library unsuccessful
188: Unit not declared in previous uses declaration
189: 'Uses' not allowed at this nesting level
190: Unit not in library
191: No private files
192: 'Uses' must be in interface section
193: Not enough room for this operation
194: Comment must appear at top of program
195: Unit not importable
201: Error in real number — digit expected
202: String constant must not exceed source line
203: Integer constant exceeds range
204: 8 or 9 in octal number
250: Too many scopes of nested identifiers
251: Too many nested procedures of functions
252: Too many forward references of procedure entries
253: Procedure too long
254: Too many long constants in this procedure
256: Too many external references
257: Too many externals
258: Too many local files
259: Expression too complicated

300: Division by zero
301: No case provided for this value
302: Index expression out of bounds
303: Value to be assigned is out of bounds
304: Element expression out of range
398: Implementation restriction
399: Implementation restriction

400: Illegal character in text
401: Unexpected end of input
402: Error in writing code file, not enough room
403: Error in reading include file
404: Error in writing list file, not enough room
405: Call not allowed in separate procedure
406: Include file not legal

APPENDIX D2
Execution Error Messages

(fatal) indicates a fatal errorr.

0	System error (fatal)
1	Invalid index, value out of range
2	No segment, bad code file
3	Procedure not present at exit time
4	Stack overflow
5	Integer overflow
6	Divide by zero
7	Invalid memory reference <bus timed out>
8	User break
9	System I/O error (fatal)
10	User I/O error
11	Unimplemented instruction
12	Floating point math error
13	String too long
14	Halt, Breakpoint
15	Bad Block

All fatal errors either cause the system to rebootstrap, or if the error was totally lethal to the system, the user will have to reboot manually. All errors cause the system to re-initialize itself.

APPENDIX D3
Input/Output Error Messages

0	No error
1	Bad block, parity error (CRC)
2	Bad unit number
3	Bad mode, Illegal operation
4	Undefined hardware error
5	Lost unit, unit is no longer on-line
6	Lost file, file is no longer in directory
7	Bad title, illegal file name
8	No room, insufficient space
9	No unit, no such volume on line
10	No file, no such file on volume
11	Duplicate file
12	Not closed, attempt to open an open file
13	Not open, attempt to access a closed file
14	Bad format, error in reading real or integer
15	Ring buffer overflow

APPENDIX D4
Differences Between UCSD Pascal and Standard Pascal

In so far as possible, "Standard Pascal" as used here means the Pascal language as defined in the new draft document that is expected to become the basis for an international standard Pascal language.

1. Case Statement

   In standard Pascal, an error is caused if none of the constants which label the controlled statements is equal to the current value of the Selector of the Case Statement. In UCSD Pascal, no error indication results from this situation, and processing simply drops through to the statement following the Case Statement.

2. Dynamic Memory Allocation

   Standard Pascal provides the built-in procedure DISPOSE(P) which indicates that the dynamically allocated variable P↑ is no longer needed. UCSD Pascal does not (yet) provide DISPOSE. Instead, the more primitive MARK and RELEASE procedures are provided.

3. Comments

   The UCSD Pascal compiler recognizes a dollar sign character ("$") in the first character contained in a comment as an indication that the comment is a directive to the compiler. Standard Pascal makes no explicit provision for compiler directives.

4. INTERACTIVE Files

UCSD Pascal augments Standard Pascal by providing the predeclared type INTERACTIVE, which is similar to type TEXT. Type INTERACTIVE simplifies handling of single character input/output to interactive terminal devices. The standard files INPUT and OUTPUT are of type INTERACTIVE in UCSD Pascal. See Chapter 8 of this book for details.

5. Random Access Disk Files

Standard Pascal contains no explicit provisions for direct random access to specific records in a disk file. UCSD Pascal augments the language with the built-in procedure SEEK, which sets the value of the current file pointer. In adition, RESET, REWRITE, GET, and PUT are redefined for disk files. See Chapter 8 of this book for details.

6. GOTO and EXIT

Standard Pascal allows GOTO to a label outside the block in which the GOTO statement appears. UCSD Pascal currently restricts GOTO to a label within the same block. UCSD Pascal provides a limited equivalent of a GOTO out of the local block by using the built-in procedure EXIT(procedure name). This is equivalent to a GOTO to a label after the last executable statement of the named procedure, which must currently be in execution.

7. Packed Variables

Standard Pascal provides the built-in procedures PACK and UNPACK for transferring data between a PACKED array, and an equivalent array which is not PACKED. Standard Pascal provides no facilities for packing and unpacking PACKED records. UCSD Pascal does not provide PACK and UNPACK, as of yet, but does permit direct assignments of value to refer to the components of a PACKED record. UCSD Pascal does not permit a component of a PACKED array or record to be used as a VAR parameter.

8. Procedural and Functional Parameters

Standard Pascal permits the identifier of a procedure or function to be passed as a parameter. This permits one procedure (or function) to use another that has been passed in as a parameter. UCSD Pascal does not yet provide this facility.

9. Program Headings

UCSD Pascal will accept the Standard Pascal form for the program heading, which includes a list of files in the form of parameters. However, UCSD Pascal does not require this list of file names, and does nothing with the list if it is provided.

10. Segment Procedures

UCSD Pascal permits one to declare a SEGMENT procedure or function, thus causing the procedure or function to be treated as overlayable (only loaded into memory when actually in use). Standard Pascal has no equivalent of this concept.

11. Separately Compiled Units

UCSD Pascal allows a collection of procedures, functions, and related CONST, TYPE, and DATA declarations to be compiled separately into a *unit*. The Unit can then be used by other programs without the need to recompile. Standard Pascal contains no equivalent of this concept. See Chapter 9 of this book for details.

12. Sets

UCSD Pascal limits a variable of type SET to have at most 4080 elements. Most other implementations of Pascal limit the number to 64 or less. Standard Pascal does not specify how many elements a set must have.

13. String Variables

UCSD Pascal provides the predeclared type STRING for working with sequences of characters. A variable of type STRING is equivalent to a PACKED ARRAY [1 . . upper-bound] OF CHAR, with a hidden length byte also included. String variables are supported with the built-in procedures INSERT and DELETE, and the builtin functions LENGTH, POS, COPY, and CONCAT. Assignment statements and comparison operations use only the number of characters in a string as indicated by the length byte, and do not require that the full declared length of the packed array be present. READ and WRITE are also extended to refer directly to string variables. Standard Pascal specifies no equivalent to type STRING.

14. Long Integers

UCSD Pascal allows the use of integers up to 36 decimal digits long. This requires the programmer to specify the number of digits desired if the size of the integer is to be longer than the size supported by the computer's processor (usually 16 bits on small machines).

APPENDIX E
INDEX

Note: Items containing "(' as second character are commands or command options. Items with lowercase first character are generic.